Ghosts of Bay City, Saginaw, and Midland, Michigan

Lisa Hoskins

Schiffer Publishing Ltd.

4880 Lower Valley Road, Atglen, Pennsylvania 19310

Schiffer Books are available at special discounts for bulk purchases for sales promotions or premiums. Special editions, including personalized covers, corporate imprints, and excerpts can be created in large quantities for special needs. For more information contact the publisher:

Published by
Schiffer Publishing Ltd.
4880 Lower Valley Road
Atglen, PA 19310
Phone: (610) 593-1777
Fax: (610) 593-2002
E-mail: Info@schifferbooks.com

Please visit our web site catalog at
www.schifferbooks.com

We are always looking for people to write books on new and related subjects. If you have an idea for a book, please contact us at the above address.

This book may be purchased from the publisher. Include $5.00 for shipping. Please try your bookstore first. You may write for a free catalog.

In Europe, Schiffer books are distributed by:
Bushwood Books
6 Marksbury Ave.
Kew Gardens
Surrey TW9 4JF
England
Phone: 44 (0)208 392-8585
Fax: 44 (0)208 392-9876
E-mail: Info@bushwoodbooks.co.uk

Website: www.bushwoodbooks.co.uk
Free postage in the UK. Europe: air mail at cost. Try your bookstore first.

DEDICATION

I would like to dedicate this book to the spirits who contributed in some way, whether they took part in this unwillingly or willingly. I continue to be respectful of you and am honored each time you let me take a glimpse into the other side.

ACKNOWLEDGMENTS

I would like to thank everyone who lent me the support I needed to write this book. If it were not for the encouragement from family and friends, I might not have had the guts to get it written at all. I would also like to thank everyone in my paranormal group for putting up with my endless talk about the book as I was working on it, and for lending a helping hand with the investigations for it. Without you, I couldn't have shared it with the perspective that I envisioned from the beginning. I would especially like to thank Bill and Sandra, who assisted me with taking pictures and for so graciously allowing me to use them, and for traveling with me for the 'day trips' that we took during the research phase.

I would also like to personally thank each person who allowed my paranormal group to come and investigate at their location and share their story because, without you, this would not have been possible. I would also like to acknowledge Troy Taylor for giving me permission to use his article, Patrick Burns for writing my book's Foreword, the Livingston Arts Council, for being so supportive, and Sharon Fisher for sharing her personal experiences. Special thanks also goes to the family where George resides, and for letting me share your story with the world.

To Fred Welsh from the Bay City Historical Society; thank you for the ghost walk tour that became my guiding light for locations in the book. You have a knack for storytelling and each ghost walk you conduct will fill those present with chills and thrills!

I would also like to acknowledge Joey Ward, for giving me the name of his publisher and telling me how his book writing process began, and to Dinah Roseberry, my editor, who never once laughed at any of the stupid questions I asked her during the whole process. Thanks Dinah!

—Lisa Hoskins

CONTENTS

FOREWORD
BY PATRICK BURNS

As someone who has had a life-long interest in the paranormal, I'm amazed at where ghost hunting (or simply "ghosting") has come from and gone to in just a few short years. When I started with my first paranormal research group in the late 1990s, this hobby was still something that was more apt to elicit a wide-eyed stare and a "You do WHAT?" response. I kept my hobby on the down-low at my various places of employment back then, though admittedly being on the 10:00 news around Halloween every year all but guaranteed I'd be the topic of water cooler talk around the office for at least the next week. Today, thanks to the media and success of such shows as "*Ghost Hunters*," "*A Haunting*," and my personal favorite, "*Haunting Evidence*" (I'm biased, what can I say?), the lay person's idea of ghost hunting and the paranormal no longer seems as off-the-wall and "weird" to the average person. In fact, in a 180 degree turn, it's now looked at by many as an endearing trait and a great conversation starter.

People are much more familiar with what we do today, and are more likely to find it fascinating and ask many questions, instead of slowly backing away and suggesting we see a shrink! The field of paranormal research is a true grass-roots movement. While not a science (yet), it's encouraging to watch the field evolve. I can only imagine the scientific minds of Copernicus, Galileo, Sir Isaac Newton, and many others who went against the grain of what was accepted "scientifically" in their day feeling the same. Only a few short years ago, most ghost hunters accepted the notion that so-called "orbs" —spherical, semi transparent objects in photographs—were definitive evidence of a spirit world.

Today, most investigators know, of course, that airborne particulate matter such as dust and pollen, humidity, and even insects are usually the culprits when we see these strange looking anomalies appear in our photos and video. Today, we are more apt to dismiss them entirely, or at the very least cast a strong skeptical eye towards them. Thus, our field is evolving. We are learning and moving forward, and while many in the established scientific community might still snicker at us, we persevere and continue on, remembering that the very same legends of science they idolize were once ridiculed by the status quo of their day as well. I find it unfortunate that very little if any academic research funds are earmarked for study of the paranormal. Most grants are, of course, given to fields that promise a tangible return on investment. Fields such as electronics, pharmaceuticals, aerospace, et al usually are the benefactors of public and private grant money. Establishing concrete evidence of a spirit world or another plane of existence would be great for humanity from a spiritual perspective, however, I doubt it would prove profitable to anyone other than established religions—who would probably use such evidence to coerce more people into the pews once a week. Thus the state of the union of paranormal research is one that is almost entirely independently funded and carried out by weekend ghost chasers.

One of the challenges any grass roots movement faces is a lack of universally-accepted standards and information. Oftentimes, I'm asked by newcomers to our field "Where are the cool haunted locations around here?" There is a great deal of information available pertaining to locations that are allegedly haunted if one looks for it; many "haunted guidebooks," both in print and online, are available. Unfortunately, many of them are merely a recital of every collected ghost story the author could find in a particular location. There is often little if any research done at these locations to verify if the reports are historically factual, or merely local "urban legend" passed down over generations, or sometimes even fabricated in much more recent times. That is where a book such as the one you are holding comes into play.

The locations you will read about within have been individually investigated by P.R.I.S.M. While no one can ever say that a location is definitively "haunted," these locations have shown promise to team P.R.I.S.M. as having highly unusual activity associated with them which seems to coincide with historical reports. While there may not be as many locations listed within this book as some other published works, I believe the old saying "quality over quantity" applies here. These are locations that have been thoroughly investigated by an established paranormal research organization and appear to have some substance to their haunted history. Check them out for yourself and see if your own experiences don't agree with their findings!

—*Patrick Burns*
Paranormal investigator of Tru TV's *"Haunting Evidence"*

INTRODUCTION
GHOST WALK
THE BEGINNING

As a paranormal investigator and founder of my own group, PRISM (short for Paranormal Researchers in Southeastern Michigan), it is only natural that I would want to share a few ghost stories with the rest of the world. As a paranormal investigator, who wouldn't? It is a part of what we love to do. As a group, PRISM loves to investigate historical buildings and landmarks because of the amount of history and emotions that are connected to these locations. We also investigate houses for people needing our help, but because historical locations are always so fascinating, it is something we cannot pass up. I chose to write about the Bay City and Saginaw areas because of the rich amount of history that is steeped into the land. Native Americans, lumberjacks, sailors on ships, the mafia and crime bosses, and the underground railroad are all embedded into these locations. As I read about some of the local urban legends, I knew that I had to investigate further, then share my findings.

I also immediately knew that I wanted my group to be a part of the whole process, and that the help would be invaluable to me, making it a group effort. My goal was to investigate the locations as a group and post our evidence on our website so you can not only read about the spooky stories here, but you can actually see any photo evidence, EVPS, or video that we captured. I will tell you a wonderfully creepy story, and then back it up with evidence of spirit activity. This book was written by someone who loves the spirit world, has great respect for the spirit world, and wants to share everything she knows about the spirit world with you. Whether you just love ghost stories that make you hide beneath your bed covers on a dark and foggy night, or you are a seasoned investigator, I hope you enjoy the book and the evidence that I and my group will be sharing with you.

Since I live over an hour away from the Bay City area, I knew my research would include trips up to the city to research stories. I told my group members that I wanted to investigate any claims of paranormal activity myself and enlisted their help. One sunny day early in August, Sandra, Bill, and I drove up to Bay City to start our new adventure. We started with a ghost walk through downtown Bay City. The tour was conducted by Fred Welsh, a volunteer for the Bay City Historical Society.

Fred began the tour at the corner of Water Street and Third. This portion of town is along the Saginaw River next to the St. Lawrence Brothers candy store, once the site of the European Hotel, which I will discuss in later chapters of this book. He led us to the large dock on the water which overlooks the river and two bridges, one on each side. The dock sits right next to the

The corner of Third and Water Streets where the St. Laurent Brothers candy store, once the European Hotel, now sits. *Courtesy of Bill Kittle.*

Kingfish Restaurant and Tiki Lounge, site of the old Wolverton Hotel. Our group of twenty or more people listened intently as Fred began the tour with stories of the Native American people who once lived along the river.

Since my first trip to Bay City involved the ghost walk where Fred began with Native American stories, I thought it fitting to begin with Native American lore. The first chapter will share the stories related to these ancient and often misunderstood people who lived and thrived along the Saginaw River, and who still might roam there even today in spirit form.

AUTHOR NOTE

From the time I decided to write this book, I knew that I wanted to make this an interactive process for you, the reader; and it was my intention from the beginning to take each of you with me on this journey into the paranormal world. Since my group has helped me with the investigations and the gathering of evidence, I've made available that evidence on our web site, so at any time you are reading the stories related here, you can go to our site at the same time and listen to audio recordings, and view pictures or video evidence that we captured. This will be beneficial for you, whether you are a ghost hobbyist or a seasoned investigator.

Additionally, you will find definitions of paranormal terms along the way and a comprehensive list at the end of the book. Enjoy your journey of ghosts, legends, and lore where you can listen to spirits speak from the other side and read the amazing stories that surround these Michigan towns.

To hear EVPs visit our website at www.ghostprism.com. You will find a collection of our EVPs under our investigations section. If you click on the appropriate location per the story you are reading, you will find the EVPs taken during that investigation. If you run into problems, please contacts me via email listed on the site and I will guide you in the right direction.

1

NATIVE AMERICAN LORE

ABORIGINAL SPIRITS OF BAY CITY

Ottawa, Chippewa-Ojibwa, and other Native American Indians lived along the banks of the Saginaw River at one time. Archaeological digs in Bay City have shown that Indians lived on the land as far back as 3000 B.C. To this day, their remains, along with artifacts, can be found along the river banks, and often times when new buildings are being built and the construction begins, the proper authorities are contacted to examine remains that are found beneath the soil on this ancient land. One story that Fred described, during the ghost walk that sunny day in August, actually made me gasp. As a strong believer in Native American culture and traditions (mostly Lakota traditions), I know how sacred certain things are in their culture. Included in this sacred circle is their strong belief in how their dead are handled. Special burial ceremonies mark the passage of someone who has died, and these ceremonies are considered to be very holy events.

To move or remove remains without proper prayers and respect is something that is unheard of in their culture. Knowing this information can be difficult when you hear stories of how their remains are sometimes handled in today's society, even now. Each time I hear a story of bones being found and then tossed or disregarded, my whole body shudders at the thought. I was, however, happy to learn that Bay City contacts the proper authorities when they find such remains, but as always,

A Native American headstone located in Elm Lawn Cemetery in Bay City.

sometimes things can slip through the cracks. Here is one such story of that happening.

DON'T TAKE MY BONES!

Location & History

In 1971, the Fletcher site in Bay City was added to the National Register of Historic Places. The National Register has it listed as 'prehistoric, historic, aboriginal' with the cultural affiliation being listed as 'late archaic, Woodland, Hopewell' (National Register of Historic Places. Site No. 71001018, 1971, Fletcher Site, www.nps.gov/history/nr). The period of significance that they list is from 1000-2999 B.C., all the way up to 1824. The sub-function is listed as a village site with graves and burials, and its current location is underwater. At one time, this location was obviously not under water, but today that is the case. It is called the Fletcher site because it is the location of the old Fletcher Oil property which now sits under a bridge along the river bank.

The Unthinkable

Forty years ago, while digging along this section of the river on the old Fletcher site, people would find artifacts left from the aboriginal people like buttons, old coins, and even bones. This was indeed the site of an old Indian camp where the mound builders, as they are called, had buried their dead. They were given the name mound builders because they buried their dead on mounds that were piled up from the ground.

As Fred, our tour guide that day, told about the Fletcher site story, my stomach began to tie in knots. He said, "Someone picked up a bone and took it home with them." I gasped! *Took it home!* I thought. I was cringing as I almost began to sweat, hearing that someone could have been so disrespectful of another person's remains. Sandra knew how I felt as she looked over at me right after Fred told us about this atrocity. Curiosity in these cases in understandable, but to take someone's bones home is a disgrace, as far as I am concerned, especially knowing the culture of these ancient people.

The person who took this bone home had it for quite some time according to Fred. Then when it was decided that it was no longer wanted, the individual gave it to the daughter of the family. The daughter, a more perceptive person when it comes to spirits and ghosts, ended up seeing an apparition at the foot of her bed. Fred didn't say whether the apparition was male or female, but I heard rumors that it was indeed the spirit of a Native American woman. It wasn't specified just what happened after the ghostly figure appeared at the end of the daughter's bed, but I imagine that the spirit was appearing to tell her to please put the bones back where they were originally buried. Hopefully, that's exactly what she did. Note to the wise: Don't take anyone's bones!

The Manesous

Is the Saginaw Valley Haunted?

During the time that Chippewas and Pottawatomies inhabited much of southern Michigan, the Sauks occupied the Saginaw river and the central areas. Known by the Chippewa as "Manesous, or bad spirits in the form of Sauk warriors," they were feared by all. The Sauks were feared so greatly, that if word got out they were near, the Chippewa people would flee their villages leaving food, clothing, and other items behind. Knowing this, the Sauks would hover around the villages and frighten them into leaving. When they did, the Sauks would take over the land that was left behind.

Getting tired of the Sauks, the Chippewas, Pottawatomies, and other tribes decided to band together and try to drive the Sauks out once and for all. They met at Mackinac Island and then started out in canoes towards their enemy, breaking up into smaller groups so they could circle them. The men on the west side of the bay left their canoes and started on foot, later attacking the main village and killing most of the village's people. Some of the men went across the river and others went to Skull Island, which is now called Stone Island. Others went to another village in Portsmouth, meeting the men who had come up the east side of the Bay, and once again finding their enemy, a large battle took place on the land. Then they retreated back to Skull Island, thinking that they were safe because the Sauks didn't have canoes. In the middle of the night, it was so cold that the river water froze over solid and the Sauks went after the other men, slaughtering everyone except for twelve families.

Do the spirits of these brave warriors still roam the Saginaw Valley today? Perhaps if you take a walk down by the river's edge, you might be able to hear the cries of the warriors who lost their lives in order to defend themselves and their families against the 'bad spirits' that they superstitiously believed had come back to haunt them. Is the land haunted? You can decide that for yourself...But I think it is.

2

HAUNTED HOUSES

I f you have never heard unexplained noises like footsteps or banging noises in your home, had lights go on or off with no explanation, or felt a cold shiver run down your back, chances are you might know someone else who has. Paranormal activity can occur in houses for a number of reasons, but during investigations with my paranormal group, the biggest reason seems to be that a previous homeowner or someone who once lived on the land is still around for whatever reason.

Strong connections to the house or land bring about strong emotions in a spirit, which in turn, can trigger paranormal activity. Tragic or untimely deaths can also account for a spirit who is not willing or is unable to cross over to the other side. Most of the time, the spirit doesn't mean any harm, they just want attention or help with unfinished business. But having any type of paranormal activity in your home can certainly be a frightening experience when you don't know who or what you are dealing with.

I and my group do our best to help any homeowner who calls with a reported haunting, and I always tell folks that I am there for them whenever they need me, even long after we have completed an investigation. Oftentimes, it takes more than one investigation to get to the bottom of things, and sometimes we enlist the help of a psychic to help put the puzzle pieces together. Some groups disagree with using psychics, stating they aren't scientific enough and the information from them cannot be validated. In my opinion, nothing in the paranormal field is scientific and has more to do with the spiritual side of things than anything else, therefore, I find psychics to be a valuable tool. If it will help the homeowner, I am all for it.

Some of the cases you will read about in this chapter are actual investigations done by me and my team. Others are experiences that were shared with me either by the person who experienced it, or someone who heard about it. For the cases that we investigated, as I mentioned earlier, I will share any evidence that was collected during our investigation. In the case of EVPS (electronic voice phenomena), more commonly known as spirit voices caught on tape, you can listen to the audio recordings yourself. I hope that this will not only educate you about paranormal activity, but will add a bit more detail to the stories. Real names and exact locations are left out of the book to protect the privacy of the people in the stories.

WHERE'S GEORGE?

In a rural area just outside of Bay City is a ranch home that sits in an area of farmland. The house isn't old by most standards, and nothing about it would indicate that it is filled with an abundance of spirit activity. This proves the point that a house does not have to be old or abandoned to be a location where paranormal activity can occur.

Ryan and Julia live a normal life not unlike many other young couples, with two children, working daily jobs, and trying to have a good family life at home. They have two sons, the youngest being two years old. Here is an excerpt of the email that Julia sent me back in January of 2007:

> *The run down is, that our house seems to be haunted by a local ghost by the name of George who we believe actually resided in the Pinconning area. (We've talked to a medium who helped to give us a bit of background regarding our ghost.) We have many strange things that occur here, names and initials written on the walls and doors in a greasy black*

substance…Noises that occur with no explanation, such as a child crying, a woman screaming, thumping under the floor and whooshing white noise type of noises. There have been objects that move on their own, such as the chandelier swinging back and forth, doors slamming shut, frames falling off of the wall, etc. Things are constantly disappearing. Money, keys, wallets, purses etc…and most often the missing items turn up in the garage cellar. Often, my twenty-two month old son's toys will be moved in the middle of the night, or toys will go off simultaneously in the playpen. My son also sometimes laughs and talks to someone who isn't there. Well, not to say it isn't there, but you know what I mean.

I contacted Julia back by email, and received another email from her saying that they had been staying at her mother-in-law's house for the weekend because after she had emailed me the first time, she had an unsettling experience in the house. Julia had been sitting on her couch in the living room, which is right next to the dining room. She heard a noise to her right side and when she looked to see what it was, she saw that the dining room table was upside down, and all four chairs were in tact, also upside down. She said that the amount of noise from this was minimal, and having a table and four chairs turn upside down all at once should have made more noise than it had. I certainly agreed with that. There had been an envelope on the table also, containing her husband's driver's license and a few other important documents that he had put in the envelope for safe keeping because they kept disappearing. He thought by placing them in the envelope, they wouldn't vanish. Right after Julia glanced over to see what had happened to the table, she also noticed that the envelope was on the floor, and on fire. She quickly put the fire out and saved what was in the envelope. Note: The PRISM team was shown what was in that envelope at a later date and the edges of Ryan's driver's license was indeed charred from the fire.

Oddly enough, that weekend at Ryan's mom's house proved to be interesting also. His mother said that a box appeared on her bed out of nowhere, and she had no idea

The outside of the wooden box that Julia's mom found in her bed with the initials G.M. and a date of 1903 carved into it.

The inside of the wooden box that contained two photos, an old plastic doll, a 1903 coin, and a piece of old broken jewelry.

where it had come from. The wooden box contained an old coin from 1903, a picture of a woman, a picture of a child, an old key, and a little plastic doll. The box had the initials GM carved on the outside along with a date of 1903. Where had this box come from, and why did it appear at Ryan's mom's house instead of at their house? Strange indeed! We have never figured out why this happened, other than the fact that a spirit knows where you are—wherever you are— and this spirit knew that the family had been staying there for the weekend. Officially, objects that manifest from a non-physical reality to a physical reality are known as apports. They are usually linked with psychic mediums during trance communications. I have never experienced an apport myself or knew anyone who had, until this investigation. This was not the only time it occurred, it was only the beginning.

THE INVESTIGATION

One cold day in February, the PRISM team did the initial investigation at this house. I must say that because of the weird events that Julia kept telling me about, I was a bit apprehensive. I had never been on an investigation where so much paranormal activity had been reported, but at the same time, I knew that this family needed help—if nothing else but to have someone to listen to their feelings about what was going on. Most people are afraid to tell their friends or family, out of fear of them thinking that they are *off their rockers*. I try to convey to each person asking us for help that we will not make fun of them or wonder if they are crazy—we are there to *help them*. This isn't to say that we don't have to take precautions. Some people will actually make up stories just to try and have someone come to their house to investigate. I have never understood this at all, but I hear of it happening.

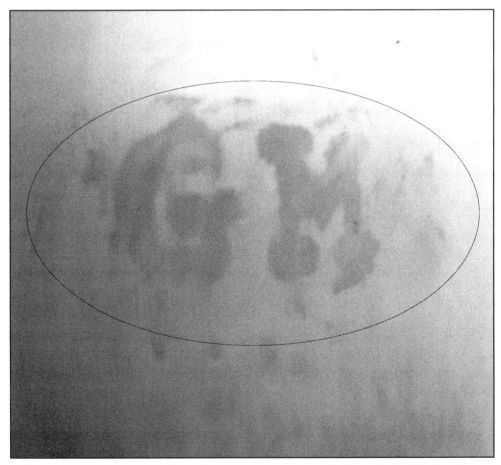

Between the time that Julia first emailed me and our first investigation, I spoke with her often because activity seemed to pick up after she'd contacted me. Numerous emails were sent back and forth and we talked on the phone more than once because of this. Just before we arrived the first time, Julia told me that a slimy substance that also felt greasy appeared on the door in the dining room that leads out into the garage. Previously, the name Meddaugh appeared on some paneling in another area of the house and was written in a black substance. Even after washing it, it had left an imprint and you can still see the letters on the paneling.

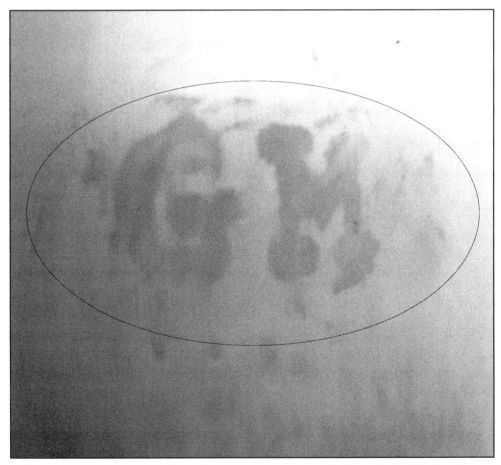

The door in the garage that leads into the dining room with the initials G.M. that had appeared as an oily substance. *Courtesy of Bill Kittle.*

We arrived at the house and had Julia and Ryan walk us through to show us where the majority of activity seemed to be taking place. They also showed us the door with the slimy clear substance on it. It started at the top of the door and flowed down the door and even on the wall next to the door. It looked mostly clear and seemed to be thick. You could see little droplets that had fallen and they would eventually stop in various spots on the door and down the wall. We took pictures of the door and of the paneling in the other room where the name Meddaugh had been written. As reported to me in Julia's first email, she told me a psychic said a spirit named George from the Pinconning area was in their house. She did some research into local records and found a George W. Meddaugh who had resided in Pinconning with his family. The information came from a 1920 census and is verifiable, because I found the same information when I did my own search for records. If you remember the initials from the wooden box, they were G.M. Coincidence or not?

At this time, I feel it is necessary to include something that happened with our group during the time we investigated at this house and the reason for fact checking and usage of multiple tools when dealing with the paranormal. A psychic we knew well went on the investigation with us. This person seemed to be dead on when it came to certain information, and at other times, I seriously doubted what I was hearing. Most of what I felt was my own intuition, which I chose to ignore to give this psychic the benefit of the doubt. Looking back, I should have trusted my gut feelings. Information was relayed to Julia and Ryan, along with my group, about the spirit activity that was going on in the house. Later, while doing some research, I discovered that this information had been taken from an old horror movie. This movie's storyline was given as fact for what was going on in this house. While searching one particular name given during this investigation, I ran across a web site that had information about this movie.

Everything the psychic had said, word for word, was there on the web site in black and white. I was in shock. Major shock. I called Julia to tell her what I'd discovered. I felt that she needed to know the truth as well as have an apology from me and an explanation that I had nothing to do with it. Luckily, she understood and was very gracious when I told her. I feel the need to explain what happened because it relates to some experiences that happened after we left the house the first time. It was a sad thing having someone do what this particular psychic did, but all things happen for a reason, and the lesson for me was to never doubt my own gut feelings. Lesson learned. Now on to the rest of the story.

Armed with our cassette recorders, digital recorders, digital cameras, laser thermometer, and EMF (electro magnetic field) reader, we started our investigation. Nothing of a paranormal nature happened that day in the way of moving objects, noises, or anything else out of the ordinary, but a few people in the group felt sick or disoriented when we first arrived. We investigated all rooms in the house as well as the garage, because one of the main problems they were having was missing keys and objects that would end up in the garage. In the garage is an old cellar that looks more like a storage area with a dirt floor. It has a wooden door that swings up to open it, and it measures approximately six foot by four foot. They always seemed to find their keys in the cellar or somewhere else in the garage, like an old microwave or a box used for storage. The keys went missing quite often, and sometimes they would disappear *while* they were in their pockets. More than once they were stranded in the house because all of the keys had come up missing. Strange I know, and almost hard to believe at times. Like I said, this was certainly nothing like I had ever heard about before.

EVIDENCE

Even though we didn't experience anything in the way of moving objects or noises, we did capture quite a few

The cellar in the garage where the family's keys, toys, and other items would appear after coming up missing in the house.

EVPs from the house. The thing about EVPs is that most times you don't hear the spirit voices with your ears because of the higher vibration that spirits are on. You hear the voices after you get home and decide to review your audio recordings. The first time we were at the house, we captured a total of eight EVPs on audio. (Visit PRISM website at www. ghostprism.com. Click on Investigations section. Click on Bay City House.)

The EVPs, along with detailed information about each one is on the web site, but I will highlight a few of them here for you to read about before you go and take a listen for yourself. In the first EVP, I was talking to Julia and her mother-in-law about the psychic mentioned earlier. As I am talking, you can hear a whisper over top of my voice that says:

"Get out now."

Many times, spirits will talk over top of you or join in on your conversations. We find that this is the most common form of EVP that we end up capturing. Some groups prefer to remain quiet while doing audio recordings, and while quiet conditions are a good thing, I don't believe that complete silence is needed. If a spirit is active, meaning not a residual energy that is left over from a past event or time, they want to communicate. They can do it much easier if they have someone to communicate with, so if you aren't saying anything, the chances of them saying anything aren't as great. This is, of course, my personal opinion, but our experience seems to back it up.

Another spirit voice that we captured on tape that day confirms the theory that spirits know who *we* are, even when we don't know who *they* are. PRISM member Sandra was walking back into the house and up the stairs from the garage when she captured an EVP that says:

"Sandy's here."

Now I suppose the spirit could have been talking about another spirit present in the home, but chances are, this is not the case. Bill, Sandra's husband, was walking out into the garage from the dining room. As soon as he got into the garage, you can hear a male voice in a low deep voice that says:

"This bothers me."

What bothered him? Was it the fact that we were there? That Bill was walking right to the cellar area where objects were taken? Was it that they knew the psychic was misleading us that day about the ghosts that were in the house? We will never know the answers to that, but we do know that they were in the house during our first investigation.

THE AFTERMATH

After we left that day, the activity seemed to get worse during the next couple of days. One strange thing that happened was that every time I would try to email any EVPs to someone in the group, my email would act up. It wouldn't let me send them. Now I know this sounds crazy, but for one full day I could not email audio evidence to anyone. I could send out regular emails to people, but not the emails with spirit voices on audio. Later on, Sandra and Bill tried to email their EVPs to me and the computer kept saying that my in-box was full. I received the email Sandra sent me telling me it was *saying* my box was full. I replied to her "If my in-box is full, then how did I just receive the email you sent me telling me that it's full?" Finally I decided to light a white candle, say a prayer, and then try it again. It worked. In the end, Sandra ended up having to use the same method. I don't know if it was a crazy coincidence or not, but it was definitely an odd experience.

Meanwhile, Julia and Ryan were experiencing what seemed to be an angry spirit who wasn't thrilled with the fact that we had come to their house to investigate. The questionable psychic actually said one thing that did happen. She said that a medal was buried in the cellar (oddly enough, this was from the movie storyline, but was true!).

A few days to a week after we were there, Julia went to make a sandwich for her younger son and pulled out a piece of bread. On the bread that had just come out of the package, the word "dig" was inscribed and looked like someone had taken their finger or a sharp object to write it. She saved the piece of bread which we saw later on. Her husband wasn't home at the time so she called him and told him what happened. He came home and she told him, "We need to dig in the cellar, Ryan."

So they started to dig in the dirt floor of the cellar out in the garage. Ryan's friend had also come back with him and he was there while they were digging. He mentioned that it might be a good idea to videotape the whole process. Ryan agreed, so he went inside to get the video camera in their bedroom. He walked to the back of the house and into their bedroom, and was facing the dresser where the video camera was when he heard a 'plop' noise. He turned to look behind him after hearing the noise, and was in shock when he noticed a small coin purse laying on their bed. It was a leather purse—the kind that has the clasp that you have to push with your thumbs to open. Inside the purse was a silver charm in the shape of a heart with an inscription on it. The inscription was "All my love, Mary." By the way, on the 1920 census for George Meddaugh, his wife's name is listed as being, you guessed it, Mary.

After digging for a few hours, they did indeed find a medal. It's actually a gold-colored necklace with a medallion

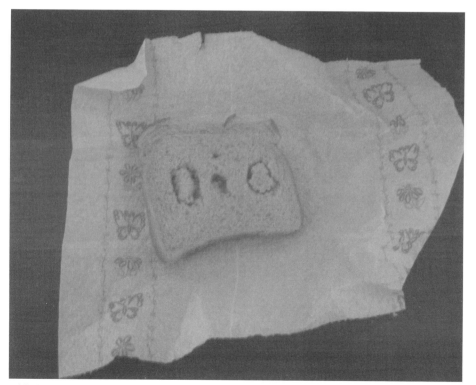

This is the piece of bread with the word DIG inscribed on it that appeared when Julia was making her son a sandwich.

that seems to be religious in nature. It looks like the Virgin Mary or another woman, with children at her feet. We took pictures of the necklace the second time that we went back to the house. The same night that the purse appeared, Julia had to go to the store to pick up a few things for the house. It was snowing lightly that night and she stated to me later on that when she came out to her car in the parking lot, the words "last chance" were written on the back of her car on the window, in the snow. This incident really seemed to bother her and the activity seemed to be getting stronger, and more strange.

I told her that perhaps the spirits knew about the psychic's misrepresented words, and they weren't happy about it. We did believe that more than one spirit was involved. We believed that George, and possibly his wife, were in the house. We also believed that there was another spirit in the house who wasn't the nicest of spirits. The psychic who had mentioned George by name prior to our visit said that he thought George's daughter needed an operation that they couldn't pay for because they didn't have the money. At this point, we wondered if George was in the house and needed help, or if his wife, Mary, was in the house and she was the one who needed help. And if they were there, what was the connection to a house that they'd never lived in? We thought that since it's in an area of farmland and he was a farmer, that maybe he rented out the land at one time to someone and a tragic event happened on the land. We couldn't find any information to support that theory.

ONE MORE TIME

I really felt we owed it to the family to go back again for another investigation. I told Julia that, while I am somewhat psychic myself, I am not a psychic with stronger abilities just yet. I thought that if we did a prayer together and tried to get the spirits to leave, they would. I just knew that I felt bad

The photo of the coin purse that appeared on Julia and Ryan's bed out of nowhere (also known as an apport) the night they were told to 'dig'. *Courtesy of Sandra Kittle.*

The gold-colored medallion necklace which was found in the garage cellar the same night the word DIG appeared in the bread and the coin purse apport appeared in the bedroom. *Courtesy of Sandra Kittle.*

for them, and so did the other members of the group. Julia herself has moments of psychic ability, as do most people, and spirits can be attracted to people who they know can communicate with them—another possibility for what was going on in their house. Sometimes she would hear a word or get a feeling, and Ryan's mom thought that the activity in the house might be connected to her daughter-in-law because of it.

We went back to the house in early March for a second go at it, this time with the intention of having a prayer circle to try to rid the spirits from the home. Julia had told me that a few days before we got there, something else had happened—well, two things actually. The first was her discovery of the word 'help' written in the carpet in their bedroom, from *underneath* the carpet. Next to the word *help* laid her keys, which had been missing for quite a while. She showed us the carpet when we got there, telling us, "Ryan and I have walked over it for two days, and I even vacuumed over it and the word is still there—weird." I stooped down to get a better look, running my hands over the word. She was right; it was coming from underneath the carpet. I looked for seams in the carpet but couldn't find a single one. I knew that the family had not done this themselves, and it made me wonder who was asking for help.

The second incident that Julia told me about involved her youngest son, whom she heard say "broken" while he was in his crib in his bedroom one night. She thought that maybe something had fallen down in his room, but when she investigated, she didn't see anything. She glanced into her bedroom and discovered that a photo of her and Ryan was on a blanket on their bed, shattered into little pieces. Next to the broken picture were the words "GO LEAVE" in a crusty, dried-up substance. The picture had been on their dresser and was not broken before this happened.

During our second visit, we did take along a few pieces of equipment like cameras and our audio recorders. I wanted to record during the prayer circle to see if we could pick

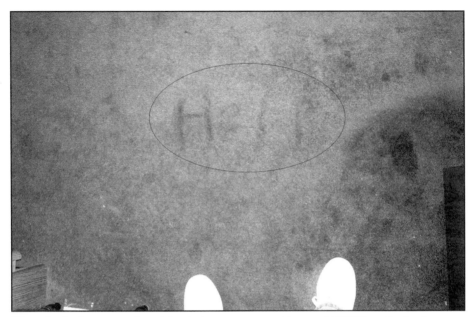

If you look close enough at this photo, you can see the word HELP on the bedroom carpet. When this originally showed up, Julia's keys (which had been missing for days) were laying next to the word.

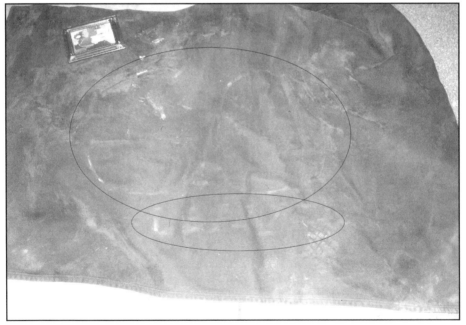

You can see the words GO (shown in the larger of the circles) and LEAVE (in the smaller circle) on the blanket, along with the broken photo which had been in a frame and on the couple's bedroom dresser before showing up on the blanket, shattered into pieces. Luckily, Julia saved this for us to look at when we came to investigate.

up spirit activity while we prayed or talked to the spirits. Julia and Ryan's friend was present at the house also, and I told them, "The more the merrier; we need more energy for this circle."

There were roughly eight people in the house that night, hoping to help Julia and Ryan rid their house of the spirits, and help the spirits to move on also. I am by no means a priest or minister, but I am a spiritual person who believes in the power of intent. I believe that it's not necessarily the tools you use for a spiritual ritual as much as it is the intent with which they are used. If a person who isn't Catholic uses holy water and doesn't have the belief or a strong intent that the water will work, will it? White sage is used by many spiritual practitioners to rid negative spirits from objects and people. Native Americans and, I believe, Pagans also, are two groups who use white sage for this purpose. I myself believe in the use of white sage as a tool, so I lit my white sage at the house and walked through the home while saying a prayer and asking for any negative energy to be removed. Again, the intent is what matters, not the tool itself.

After I used the white sage throughout the house, I asked everyone to gather in a circle in the living room so that we could start the prayer. I was very nervous about leading the circle, so I asked for some guidance from my spirit guides, Angels, and God. I lit a candle and placed it on the floor in the middle of a circle and then asked everyone to join hands. I said a small prayer of protection for everyone present, asking for us all to be surrounded and protected from any negative energy or spirits. I told everyone there that it didn't matter what their belief system was—even if they believed in a purple bunny as their God (that one got a chuckle from everyone). But my point was that as long as all of us had the thoughts of helping these spirits leave this house, the energy would be strong, no matter what each person's individual belief system was.

We believed there was more than one spirit in the house at the same time. We felt that one, or possibly two, of the spirits were harmless, while the other spirit seemed to be the one holding all of the negative energy. As I spoke to the spirits that night, I told all of them that although we were all aware of their presence, that we were unsure of exactly what they wanted help with, so we could not help them. I asked them nicely to leave the house and told them that if they crossed over into the light, they could see their family and friends waiting for them on the other side. Our main concern was for the family living in the house, but we were also concerned with getting these spirits to the other side so that they could be at peace. Even the family living in the house wanted these spirits to cross over, for the spirits' sakes, not just for their own peace of mind.

When we were done with the circle, I told Julie and Ryan that I didn't know if our circle worked or not. I only prayed and hoped that it had. It was very calm when we held the circle and we didn't experience any noise or negative activity either. A good sign? I thought so. The spirit who seemed to hold the negative energy could have made a fuss if it really wanted to, but it didn't. I told Julia to keep me informed of any activity, should they have any after that night. I kept in contact with her by email and a few times by phone also, because I was concerned about how all of this would play out in the end.

I wanted to bring a new psychic in to see what could be picked up on. I wasn't having much luck finding one I felt I could trust. Many months later, I did find one who I wanted to take into the house and told Julia about it via email. I didn't get a response from her which I thought was a bit odd at the time, but recently she told me why she hadn't responded. You see, after the night we were there and held the circle in the house, the activity dwindled down and then virtually stopped. I must admit that I was shocked to hear that they hadn't had any missing keys, writings on the walls, or any other activity anymore. Yes! It worked!

My shock turned into happiness after hearing that this family could finally lead a normal life again. The reason Julia didn't respond to my email about bringing another psychic in was, "Things have been so quiet here, that I am afraid to stir the pot up again." Totally understandable, and I agreed one-hundred percent. Taking another psychic into the house might have stirred things up again, because we don't know if the spirits crossed over, or simply stopped their pranks.

Either way, we are all very glad that it's been so quiet in the house.

THE THEORY

As I sit here and write this, the story is still unbelievable to me, and I was a part of it. I have heard many ghost stories but had never been asked for help from someone who was experiencing activity on this scale before. Do I believe what Julia and Ryan told us? Yes, most definitely. I believe they are sincere and honest people who wouldn't make things up. The first psychic she talked to mentioned the man named George, and said he was in the house. Later on, the last name Meddaugh appears written on their wall, and a box appears with the initials G.M on it. The census backed up this man's name and his wife, Mary. If you remember, the name Mary was inscribed on the locket that appeared in the coin purse at the house. From piecing together what the psychic told Julia, and from some of the EVPs that we captured while we were at the house, we believe that George and Mary were both there, or one or the other was there and wanted help. We think that their daughter might have needed an operation which they couldn't afford, and that was keeping them from crossing over. One of the EVPs taken from the house was a woman's voice saying,

"I gave it all away."

Was that Mary saying she gave all of the household money away—money they could of used for the daughter's operation? We will never know the answer to that question, but we all believe that they were there because of unfinished business or high emotional upset.

As for the other spirit who we feel was the negative energy in the house and responsible for most of the activity, we are not sure why he was there. It could be a connection to the land, and Bay City has a history of the underground railroad, so he could be connected to that as well. We do know that he didn't seem to be a very happy person from the sound of his voice and things that he said on audio, combined with the threatening things that were written on blankets and car windows such as "leave now" and "last chance." For some reason, he didn't want this family around. The fact that he didn't want them around makes me feel as if he lived on that land at one time and feels that the land is his.

When Julia searched the land records, she had a hard time finding any information dating far enough back for us to figure out the puzzle. We do all feel that he was the one causing problems in the house, and we believe that George was actually looking out for her and the kids. After things had quieted down, her young two year old, who had previously seemed to be talking to someone when nobody was there with him in his room, asked Julia, "Where's George?" Her young son not only knew his name, but acted as if he hadn't seen him, and missed him. We never felt that her son was in danger because, during the times he seemed to be talking to a spirit, he didn't cry or scream. In fact, she said there were a few times that he was actually laughing. This, along with a few other incidents, led us to believe that George was acting as a protector for the family. Could he have been protecting them from the negative spirit who was also in the house? We feel that is probably what was going on in this house.

GHOSTLY MAN IN THE MIRROR

Right in downtown Bay City sits an old white farmhouse with blue shutters and land records that date back as far as 1895. What the land records don't show are the ghostly events that took place in this house back in 2005, ultimately chasing one family out of the house.

Denise, along with her sisters, ages seven and four, and her Mom, rented out the old farmhouse back in 2005. They had no idea when they moved in that they would soon be moving back out again because they would be too afraid to stay in the house anymore. The house was charming, as are many old farmhouses, with glass doorknobs and a big glass window that sits nine feet from the ground. Wooden stairs adorned the living room leading upstairs to the bedrooms. But along with the old wooden stairs came creaking noises and heavy footsteps during the night that didn't belong to the Mom or her daughters.

NIGHTLY VISITORS

Night time seemed to be the time when most of the activity took place in the old farmhouse. Denise would wake up to hear a little child crying loudly in the middle of the night, and this happened on a regular basis. Each night at 1:30 am, the closet across the room of Angel, Denise's sister, would open and close again on its own. On one occasion, Angel awoke between 1:30 and 2:00 am saying she heard a chirping noise, and then growling. She ran to her Mom and told her, and as she did, the door slammed in Denise's bedroom, shaking the wall and causing a picture to fall from the wall to the floor.

Denise's son also lived with her in the house and was two years old. He would call out for someone named Angel, which wasn't unusual considering that his Aunt's name was Angel—except that when he called out the name, Denise's sister wouldn't be anywhere near him at the time and nobody else would be in the room. Denise thought this was odd behavior from her son and didn't believe that he was calling out to her younger sister.

One night, Denise was in the living room relaxing, when she saw the reflection of a man in the mirror. She said he walked across the room, wearing brown pants and a white shirt. He vanished as quickly as he had appeared, and after that night, Denise kept her guard up around the house. There were many times when Denise would feel as if people were watching her and her family, and she felt that someone did not want them in this house at all. The family would feel chills around them and checked the thermostat more than once, but it was always set to 70 degrees. Denise doesn't feel that the chills had anything to do with a drafty house, but more to do with whatever spirit or spirits were in the house.

THE FAMILY INVESTIGATES

Denise decided to try and investigate for herself just who or what was in the house. She set up a video camera on the wooden stairs with a light shining up the steps, because the video camera didn't have a night vision function on it. As the family sat in the living room near the stairs while the camera was rolling, they saw an orb in the bathroom, which sat at the top of the stairs. The light went off near the camera and as it did, they saw an orb move down the stairs and then disappear. Things seemed to get more intense in the house after that night when the orb was seen.

TIME TO MOVE

Denise felt as if a bug was crawling on her back one night. Then it felt like a scratch. When she looked at her back she noticed that there was a mark where she had been feeling strange sensations. After the scratch appeared on her back, the family started sleeping in the same room together, too afraid of sleeping by themselves in their own rooms. Denise also decided to use a Ouija board, hoping to find out just who was in their house. She believed that a girl was in the house who wore a white dress and had blond hair. Not too long after though, her Mom decided that enough was enough, and the family moved out of the rented farmhouse. Three years after living in this old farmhouse, Denise is a paranormal investigator with her husband and still lives in the Bay City area. The name of their group is PIM, Paranormal Investigators of Michigan.

Ǝ

HELL'S HALF MILE

THE HISTORY

ater Street in downtown Bay City runs along the Saginaw River, and between the years 1850-1900 during the lumbering days, it was also given the name "Hell's Half Mile." Transient lumberjacks who had been away for up to nine months in the forests cutting down trees for hours on end would come to Bay City by boat every May, with their hard-earned money in their pockets just waiting to be spent. These men had a few things on their minds when they would come to shore. Women, drinks, and food to name a few, and more than likely, in that order. Water Street was given the name "Hell's Half Mile" because it was one of the raunchiest streets in Bay City at the time, if not all of Michigan. In 1887, there were 81 hotels accommodating 6,000 people in Bay City and West Bay City, and in 1891, there were 232 licensed saloons. Hotels and saloons made up much of Bay City back then, and if you were a lumberjack on the loose, the saloon was the place to be.

Four thousand ships came into the river in 1872, to the edge of Water Street where the old Third Street Bridge connected east and west Bay City, divided by the Saginaw river. The old bridge sat between the old Wolverton House, now the Kingfish Restaurant and Tiki Lounge, and the European Hotel which is now the St. Laurent Brothers building, makers of peanuts and chocolate. At this time, Hell's Half Mile was home to over 47 saloons—167 of them ran along the water's edge down Water

Street. Drunken lumberjack's didn't always get along so well with each other, and so, of course, there were numerous fights between them.

Several underground tunnels ran through the streets in the area, making access to the seedy saloons a breeze. If you stand on the pier where the Third Street Bridge once stood, connecting east and west Bay City, you can see the back entrance to the St. Laurent Brothers building. I was told by Fred Welsh during the ghost walk that "They would walk under the bridge straight to the door of the building, and access the tunnels from the basement." Fred told us that it's likely that the tunnels are still there in the basement today. These tunnels lead to underground seedy locations that were dangerous for even the most seasoned lumberjack to hang out in. It wasn't uncommon to see two to three bodies floating down the river each month, victims of a drunken brawl or robbery and assault. The combined history of Native Americans who once lived along the river—some of them whose remains can still be found—and the lumberjack days of women, booze, and brawls, give way to the belief by some that the ghosts of days gone by still roam through Hell's Half Mile today.

FOURNIER'S FATE

Born in Quebec, Canada, around 1845, Fabian "Joe" Fournier came to Michigan because there was more money to be made here after the Civil War. Joe Fournier stood six feet tall in an era when most men were much shorter. He had very large hands and rumors went around that he had two sets of teeth. He was married with two children, but even they couldn't stop his love of a good fight when the mood struck him, which was often. He was one of those types of people who might beat you to a pulp if you looked at him the wrong way.

Fabian "Joe" Fournier is rumored to have been the legendary Paul Bunyan himself. Many other states and cities lay claim to Paul Bunyan, but local historians have dug deep to try to lay claim to him as the real deal. Regardless of whether this rumor is true or not, Joe was no stranger to swinging an axe and was hired as a boss logger—the man in charge of the other lumberjacks. He was said to be tough when it came to running his logging camps, and considering his size, most men obliged by his rules.

Michigan was a dry county from the years 1855-1875, but that didn't stop many of the lumberjacks who frequented Water Street. In 1875, at the end of prohibition, the men were excited to hear the good news. During this time, a ship full of lumberjacks headed towards Bay City in celebration of the end of prohibition. The rowdy lumberjacks on ship began to brawl from all the excitement. The ship docked near the old Wolverton House, and as

The Bay Antique Center, formerly the Campbell House, which sat in the heart of Hell's Half Mile. Does old Joe Fournier still roam here looking for the man who killed him so long ago?
Courtesy of Bill Kittle.

Joe Fournier walked down the old gangplank towards the old Campbell House, someone asked where he was going. Joe's

reply was, "To hell." Minutes later, a stone mason from Saginaw hit Joe in back of the head with a carpenter's mallet and killed him. Some say that Joe was just exiting the ship when he was killed, and others have him walking across the street to the old Campbell House (now the Bay City Antiques Center) when he was killed. As the story goes, the man was never convicted of the crime.

The Bay Antique Center was built in 1852 by Jonathon S, Barclay, and is three floors tall and over 60,000 square feet. During the time it was the Campbell House, it contained a post office and a hall that was used for dancing and community meetings. Legend has it that Joe still roams between the old Wolverton and the Campbell House. Rumors in Bay City state that odd noises have been reported coming from the old Campbell house on the third floor.

When Sandra, Bill, and myself spent the day in town to take the ghost walk, we also walked through this enormous antique mall. We did check out the third floor but never heard anything unusual when we were there. Just because we didn't hear anything, doesn't mean that the building is free from a ghost, or more than one ghost. Could it be that Joe still roams his old hangouts where he use to brawl with the other men, or is it just a long standing ghost legend from Bay City? You can find out for yourself by visiting the Bay Antique Center. It's located at 1010 N. Water Street at the corner of Third, right in the heart of what was before some of the roughest territory of Hell's Half Mile. If you pay the Bay Antique Center a visit, don't forget your money—they have thousands of antiques to choose from! Just don't purchase a ghost along with your new treasures...

4

DOWNTOWN GHOSTS

GHOST OF THE STATE THEATRE

Downtown Bay City is quite charming, with it's architecturally-beautiful buildings containing a history that seems to whisper as you walk past. There is a quaint and friendly feeling throughout the downtown area that seems to keep its history alive somehow. Traces of the past can be seen on many of the buildings, such as the Davison Building which use to house one of the nicest theaters in town, the Regent. There are still old remains of the theater on the outside of the building, tell-tale signs of days gone by.

Sitting diagonally across the street today is the State Theatre. Built in 1908, the State Theatre was originally the Bijou, a vaudeville burlesque house, one of many in Bay City at that time. The original design was a box-style, and was remodeled in 1930 and turned into a movie theater. C. Howard Crane, a renowned architect responsible for the design of the Fox Theaters in Detroit and Missouri, was also the one who re-designed the State Theatre. It was given a Mayan Temple theme with a gorgeous Art Deco interior. The inside of the theater is both warm and inviting.

As Fred Welsh led the ghost walk, we listened intently as he enthusiastically talked about the fateful day when the manager of both the Regent and the State Theatre was murdered in the street.

The State Theatre in downtown Bay City, complete with it's own 'ghost chair' which is reserved for the Theatre's former manger. *Courtesy of Bill Kittle.*

A glimpse of the Mayan style design inside the State Theatre.

Another photo showing the Mayan design in the hallway of the Theatre.

As the manager of both theaters, Floyd was responsible for depositing money from they day's receipts of both locations. Floyd picked up the receipts from the State Theatre, and then began walking across the street to the Regent to collect the receipts there. Putting it in Fred's words as he told the story, "Through the door of the State Theatre walked a murderer." He pointed to the door on the building.

That murderer was Johnny Woo, twenty-two at the time, in 1943. As Floyd walked out of the Regent and down the street towards the bank, receipts in hand, Johnny followed him. As Floyd stepped up to the night deposit to put the money in, Johnny Woo stuck a 32 in Floyd's back and said, "Stick em' up." Floyd's reply to Johnny was, "You're kiddin' me!" Floyd turned around to face Johnny, and Johnny shot him twice, killing him. Johnny Woos, defended by local attorney David R. Skinner, spent twenty-four years in prison, later being released in 1967 by a jury of his peers in Pontiac, Michigan.

The Rumors

As Fred ended his story about Floyd and Johnny, he told us that reports of a ghost in the theater have been spoken by some. Was Floyd still there? He also mentioned that a worker had fallen off some scaffolding during some renovations at the theater. Was the worker still hanging around?

The PRISM team wanted to find out if the claims of the ghostly activity were true, so we set out to try to investigate for ourselves. I contacted the theater in the hopes of securing an investigation, or in the least, an interview. The theater was gracious enough to grant us our request and we investigated the theater in November, shortly after Thanksgiving.

I spoke with Paul Phillips, Director of Operations for the theater. He has been involved with the theater on and off since 2003, and consistently since 2004. As I interviewed Paul, the rest of the PRISM team set up our equipment and began the investigation. Paul was very cordial to all of us and gave us full access to all of the rooms in the theater.

The inside is quite impressive, with the Art Deco style of the Mayan Temple theme inside. It is a small theater, with the main stage for the focal point and a small balcony area. The theater seats roughly 600 people and some of their current events include movies, live events, and educational programming.

As Director of Operations, Paul spends a lot of time in the theater by himself. I asked him if he has ever had a paranormal experience of his own, to which he replied that he has experienced some unusual events during times when he has been in the theater after a previous night's event, cleaning up and getting it ready for another affair. There is a door near the concession area, located in the front of the building, and to the right of the doors that take you into the main seating area. The door used to be the access to the balcony area, back before 1930 when they remodeled some of the areas. The door now leads to part of the basement, which is divided into two narrow rooms, on opposite sides of the building. Paul told me he was in the theater one night doing some work and was standing near the concession area. He was alone in the building at the time, when he heard the door to the basement open and then close on its own. The main theater doors were shut and there was no breeze to speak of, so when he heard the door open and then close on it's own, he thought it was a bit strange.

THE GHOST SEAT

There have been rumors over the years that a ghost roams the theater. I asked Paul where the reports came from, hoping I could validate them, and he thinks most of the reports have come from those involved with the theater—but he couldn't give me any exact stories of reports, only the rumor that a ghost, or more than one ghost, resides in the building. Between Floyd Ackerman's demise and the story of the man falling off the scaffolding (there is no evidence that supports a man fell off any scaffolding to his death), Paul agrees that perhaps there

might be a ghost or two in the building. So much so does the theater feel that a ghost might be there, that they dedicated a seat in the building for the ghost, whom they believe is more likely to be Floyd, the old manager of the theater.

In 2004, a metal plate was put on the arm of one of the seats in the balcony, in the section of the last row closest to the wall. Just in case you plan on taking a trip to find the ghost yourself, I will explain exactly where the seat is so you can easily locate it! If you are facing the stage while standing in the balcony, the seat is in the upper left back-row section of the balcony seating. The plate simply says, "Ghost." I asked Paul why the theater would go to so much trouble to actually dedicate a seat just for the ghost. He told me that if it is in fact Floyd, the theater wants him to know that he is more than welcome to hang out at his old workplace.

So does Floyd hang out in the theater watching shows with the rest of the current theater-goers? In the next section I will share with you a bit of our investigation and then what we found when doing our research there.

The 'ghost seat' is the chair in the last row on the far right-hand side, reserved for the Theatre's old manager, Floyd Ackerman (and any other ghost in the Theatre who would like to sit there).

OUR INVESTIGATION

After I finished interviewing Paul Phillips, I joined the rest of the team so I could do some research of my own. I spent about an hour talking with Paul and recorded the interview so I could go back over my notes later on, making sure I wouldn't miss anything in my notes.

The first place I wanted to head was the infamous ghost chair Paul had told me about during our talk. I walked straight to the balcony where I found Sandra and Bill taking pictures and doing some EVP work. Paul and Tammy, the other PRISM members present that night, were in another part of the building. As I got up to the balcony, I noticed that Sandra was actually sitting very close to the ghost chair, and we discovered it was the seat next to where she was seated. When I told them the story, she quickly got up and said she didn't want to sit in the chair reserved for the theater ghost. After she got up, I ,of course, wanted to sit right down in the chair and do some EVP work, but wanted to be polite, so I asked permission before sitting down.

As I sat, I spoke to Floyd, asking if he sat in the chair, hoping to get some hard evidence of him being in the theater. I also asked various questions towards the man who had supposedly fallen off the scaffolding. When we investigate, we do ask detailed questions, but we also like to leave our recorders on and take them with us as we go throughout the building taking pictures, video, etc. We find that we get quite a few EVPs when we talk amongst ourselves. The spirits like to join in our conversations, and we find that we usually get more EVPs this way, as opposed to asking specific questions. I hoped that we would walk away with some fabulous EVPs so we could determine if the rumors of the theater ghost(s) were true or not.

Since I had just joined everyone, Sandra said she would take me to the original section of the basement area where her and Bill had already been. The stairs leading down to this basement are a bit eerie, made of brick and they wind down in a bit of a spiral fashion. The first time I had walked down with Bill when deciding where to put one of the video cameras, I told him that I didn't care for this room at all. There are actually two adjoining rooms, connected by a door that looks more like something from the dark ages—with a rounded arch and made of metal or steel, or some other very heavy material. The door is very overwhelming and seems rather large to be in a basement area of this size. The first room is full of electrical equipment and really sets off the EMF (electro-magnetic field) readers. As you pass through that room and out the very large door that connects the rooms, you enter the second room. It's also made of brick, and is two levels, with a few steps from one level to the next. Off to the side, another little room sits, full of old bricks and cement that lay strewn out on the floor.

Sandra changed the tape on the video camera and I started taking some pictures. I told her that I still felt uneasy in the room, as I had when I was there with Bill. I wasn't sure if it was my mind playing tricks on me or not. When you are in an old dark basement that is musty and made of ancient brick, that can really mess with your mind, so it's good to keep a level head and try to remember that when investigating. I took some pictures and then started some more EVP work, asking the usual questions here and there. The more we stayed in the room, the worse I felt. I began to feel dizzy and told Sandra it was beginning to really bother me. I also had the name Robert come to me, and felt this man was either confused or lost, or both, which would account for the uneasiness that I continued to feel. While I do not call myself a psychic medium, I do have certain abilities that normally don't present themselves while we are investigating. I believe that is due to the fact that I am not in the right frame of mind (relaxed enough) to be able to focus on the spirit world. Sometimes though, the spirits decide that I should talk to them anyway, leaving me no choice. Information usually comes to me as words, and most of the time I have no idea what they mean, I just hear them.

Part of the basement in the Theatre where I felt very uncomfortable and sick during our investigation there.

On this night, in this old basement, the name Robert came to me, along with the feelings of dread I had. After about twenty-five to thirty minutes of investigating in this section, I felt so sick that I told Sandra I had to get out, so we left and headed towards the other section of the basement near the front concession area.

We continued on with our investigation, and besides myself, one other person on the team had an experience while we were there. Paul and Tammy had been up in back section of the balcony area, closer to the middle of the section, which is also pretty close to the light booth room. Paul heard what to him sounded like shuffling feet across the floor. He, of course, asked Tammy if she had heard it, and she had not. While I was downstairs interviewing Paul Phillips, Paul and Tammy walked in and told us about what Paul had heard. Paul Phillips debunked the sound for us, telling us that in the light booth on the ceiling is a round section that has a roof flap on it. He said that when the wind blows, the flap will blow back and forth, causing a sound similar to shuffling feet. Mystery solved!

We enjoyed our investigation at the theater and Paul was very cordial to us and provided a wealth of information to me during my interview. We investigated each room of the theater and although we didn't see any apparitions (none had been reported that we knew of) or experience any extreme activity, we really enjoyed ourselves.

EVIDENCE

We didn't capture anything that we believed to be of a paranormal nature in photos from the theater, but we did capture a few EVPs while we were there. (Please visit web site.) Two of the EVPs we captured were with my recorder during the time that I was interviewing Paul. Both of the EVPs came from the concession area, and Paul Phillips was speaking at the time. The first one was taken when Paul was explaining the roof flap to us, and the EVP seems to be saying "No", as he is talking about the flap. It sounds like a female who is whispering. Did she mean *no, it wasn't the roof flap, but me*? Or was she saying *no* to something else? We will never know the answer to that question.

The second EVP in the concession area is another whisper which again sounds like a female voice to me, but we are unsure what she is saying. She is talking over Paul Phillips' voice, so it's not easy to hear the words.

I have a strong faith in the fact that spirits get to know our energy. Paul is at the theater on a regular basis taking care of the building. I believe that his closeness to the building played a huge part in the EVPs that came from my recorder that night. Sandra and Bill also got two EVPs, one during the time we were setting up, and another taken from the main floor area. We had three video cameras running that night and didn't capture anything unusual on any of them.

Paul told us something very interesting just before we left that night. He said that on a daily basis, the phone constantly rings. All hours of the day and night, no matter what time it is. Many times they will call to ask about shows or ticket information. He said it usually rings off the hook, even when he is the only one in the theater. He told us it was very strange that the night we were there, the phone was ringing before we got there, but right after we walked in the door, all the way up to the time we left, the phone had not rung. Not even once. He was pretty surprised by this and couldn't get over the fact that the phone had literally stopped ringing while we were there. I also found this fascinating and said, "Well, maybe the ghost of the theater wanted to make sure that we heard him, so he stopped the phone from ringing while we were there to avoid any interruptions and noise that might hinder our investigation." Since we did capture some EVPS that night, this really could have been the reason. Paul said he couldn't remember a time when the phone just didn't ring.

CONCLUSION

Is the State Theatre in Bay City haunted? We did walk away from our investigation with about six voice recordings, so that says something. Just because we did not see any apparitions or hear any loud bangs, does not mean that there are not any ghosts in the theater. It only means that we did not personally experience them if indeed they are there. I would say that there are spirits there due to the fact that we captured some EVPS. I cannot say if Floyd Ackerman is there or not, because our questions to him remained unanswered. Perhaps that's the way Floyd wants it! To learn more about the State Theatre, go to www.statetheatrebaycity.com. Or you could always give them a call, if the line is not already in use by ghostly forces...

Old City Hall Restaurant, formerly Bay City's old City Hall building, complete with a jail in the basement. Does an old 'waiter girl' leave lumps of coal on Table 14? *Courtesy of Bill Kittle.*

OLD CITY HALL RESTAURANT

TABLE 14 ANYONE?

Construction began on a new City Hall in Bay City in 1894, and ended in 1897. That building is now listed as a Historical Landmark. It sits at 301 Washington Avenue and is still in use today as the current City Hall. The old City Hall is also on Washington, further down the road and pretty close to the State Theatre, but today it is the home of a restaurant—Old City Hall Restaurant. Fitting don't you think? The old City

Hall also housed the City Jail during the time it was used, and the new building also had space for a jail as well. The city had grown so large that the original building was just too small for the city's needs.

The old City Hall was built in approximately 1862, one block down from Hell's Half Mile—the nastiest section of town. At that time, they had one police officer for every 2,200 citizens of the city, and I feel sorry for any man who worked the streets of Bay City back in those days! Prostitutes were very common during this time, and were called 'pretty waiter girls.' They lived along Water Street by the hundreds, servicing the lumberjacks and other men who frequented Hell's Half Mile.

I first heard about the prostitutes during the ghost walk and later ran across more information while doing research. History in itself amazes me, and I can spend hours languishing in the tales of a city like this one, that used to be so rough. I often wonder how the women felt during these times, whether they were ordinary women, or 'pretty waiter girls' down by Water Street. It couldn't have been easy on them, that is for sure. As I continued with my research, I ran across more than one story of a prostitute committing suicide and I wondered if the tough life they led contributed to the rate of suicide among them. I am quite sure that it did.

Some of the prostitutes would, of course, end up in jail, right alongside the drunken lumberjacks and other men who landed in lockup. I don't even want to imagine what happened to the women once inside the jail. One story mentions a prostitute who killed herself by shooting herself with a dose of morphine while she was in one of the houses of prostitution. Supposedly, a few customers and a few doctors tried to save her, to no avail.

One of these 'pretty waiter girls' was said to have killed herself in the jail that was located in the original City Hall building. Her name was said to be Emily, but people called her

Em for short. As I heard the story told about Em, I wondered how many other prostitutes or even men had committed suicide in the old jail. During the time Fred told us the story on the ghost walk, we were standing across the street from what is now used as the restaurant. Visions of people roaming the street filled my head, along with a vision of Em, so distraught that she took her own life.

Old City Hall Restaurant features fine dining and from the outside looking in, the place seems to be very nice. You can see the round tables set up with the fine linens. (We thought of going for some dinner the day of the tour, but we ended up eating somewhere else because we didn't feel we were dressed well enough to eat in a fine dining restaurant.) We were told, however, that if we were to go in and dine at the restaurant, to ask for Table 14.

Thinking that was an odd thing to say, everyone at the tour seemed to ask at the same time, "Why Table 14?" It seems that Table 14 is the most popular table in the restaurant because it's said to be the haunted table. Workers at the restaurant had stated that lumps of coal seem to appear out of nowhere and end up at Table 14. They believe, or did believe, that the restaurant was haunted, perhaps by the spirit of Em, the prostitute who took her own life in the old jail. I myself wonder why a spirit would move lumps of coal unless they had a direct connection to coal somehow. Of course, old buildings were once heated by coal, as were houses before there was electricity. Perhaps the ghost at the restaurant is in fact Em, and she is just a playful spirit who likes to make people wonder why lumps of coal are appearing at only one table. Or maybe the spirit has a connection to that particular spot in the building for some reason. I guess the possibilities could be endless. Nevertheless, if you are ever in Bay City and want to dine at a nice restaurant, stop by the Old City Hall Restaurant and ask for Table 14 when you do. Perhaps Em will join you.

SECOND STORY WILD WOMAN

Alright, so the woman was not wild, but she did *train* wild animals, and she did it above old City Hall. If you have walked through a town that has a historical district, you will probably notice that most of the buildings are usually two and three floors high. Oftentimes, the first floor was used for something separate than the second and third floors. This is the case with the old City Hall building. The first floor housed the City Hall, but the second floor was rented out to various people over the years.

Rumor has it that this is a true story that was featured in the local paper at one time, many years ago. A woman rented out the second floor during the time the building was used as the City Hall. She was an animal trainer and would keep wild animals upstairs. Not just small wild animals—large ones, such as tigers and other wildlife. She had a large training cage that she kept, and as the story goes, I believe it was a tiger that was part of this story.

The woman animal trainer also had a helper who would come in and help feed the animals and take care of them. One day, her helper came in and as she turned her head to do something, the animal grabbed her by the head, ultimately killing her.

Since this death supposedly occurred in the old City Hall which is now the restaurant, it might lend a hand to the reports of ghostly activity coming from the restaurant. I am also guessing that there were probably other deaths that occurred there which could mean some spirits haven't crossed over yet, and are still roaming the building.

THE EUROPEAN HOTEL

The European Hotel sat on Water Street at the corner of Third, and as I previously mentioned, it is now the St. Laurent Brothers building. This building sits right at the water's edge,

A drawing of the old European Hotel, which is now the St. Laurent Brothers building. The European Hotel was home to the catacombs of Hell's Half Mile.
Courtesy of Sandra Kittle.

directly next to the pier that stands now which once was the location of the Third Street Bridge. The European Hotel was owned by F. Hopp, according to information on the historical sign that sits on the pier today. The sign also mentions the fact that the patrons would "have a ringside seat" for viewing any activity occurring down Hell's Half Mile. Because the hotel was so easily accessible from the bridge, this is where many of the lumberjacks and other travelers would end up drinking and slumbering. The lumberjacks would come into shore at the Third Street Bridge, walk under the bridge and then directly into the hotel, or into one of the catacombs that was accessible from the basement of the building. There is no doubt that many a lumberjack perished in the building from either a drunken brawl or from being murdered by another lumberjack or local

man. These were daily occurrences along Hell's Half Mile during early times.

THE BOY WITH THE BALL

I spoke with an employee at St. Laurent Brothers on the phone one day, and she informed me that some of the older employees have spoken about seeing a little boy ghost in the building. She said that they have seen him playing with a blue ball upstairs on the third floor, which is now used mainly for storage space. The second floor is used for production of the products that they sell, like the roasted peanuts and chocolates. I have personally been in the building and didn't see a boy ghost with a blue ball. Then again, I wasn't on the third floor. If you would like to see the building, take a trip to Bay City during the summer months and stop into the St. Laurent Brothers building for some ice cream or chocolate. Their ice cream is wonderful, and you might just see the little boy while you are there. You never know!

5

HAUNTED CEMETERIES

When people are looking to find ghosts, it seems that the first place they head is their local cemetery. Society and media have played a part in the notion that all cemeteries are haunted locations, and if you go after dark, you might see the image of a woman in white walking between gravestones, looking for her family or upset that she was killed by a car on the nearby road. It seems that nowadays, every town and city have stories of cemeteries, roads or bridges that include a woman in white. I always joke with my team and say, "Why are they always in white; why isn't she dressed in purple, or black?!" I believe the stories always have her dressed in white because people have the misconception that all spirits would wear white. I also do not believe that so many cemeteries have a woman in white roaming near or through them. I think that sometimes, stories can get blown out of proportion, especially after they travel from person to person. With the Internet so readily available in this day and age, you can do a simple search for your city and it wouldn't surprise me if you had your own woman in white. The tri-cities area of Bay City, Saginaw, and Midland are no exception to the famous woman-in-white story. Saginaw even has a white car that goes along with the woman in white!

DICE ROAD CEMETERY, SAGINAW

If you live in the Saginaw area, you might be one of the people who have been brave enough to roam through Dice

Cemeteries can be ghostly—under the right conditions.

Road Cemetery at night, looking for the woman in white. This particular cemetery is reported to be so scary that some people refuse to step foot in it.

Down the road from the cemetery is a one-lane bridge that has quite a creepy story attached to it as well. As the story goes, a warlock was upset because a couple of girls stepped on his wife's grave. The warlock lived right next to the cemetery and saw the girls walk over his wife's grave, sending him into an angry fit of rage, ultimately getting revenge by hanging ropes from their necks and throwing them over the guardrail. People have seen a white car following them while they drive near or over the one-lane bridge, while trails of puffy white mist and smoke lingered in the night sky.

A friend of mine told me about this cemetery and I did some research, which led me to the stories about the warlock and woman in white. My friend stated to me that many of her friends have had eerie and weird experiences in the cemetery and she herself took a trip to the location, but she said she didn't experience anything out of the ordinary when she was there. Being the curious person that I am, I told my team that we needed to check out this cemetery for ourselves to see if the ghostly tales of the woman in white and the haunted one-lane bridge were true. We went out during the latter summer months and did our investigation.

The cemetery is commonly called Dice Road Cemetery by the locals, but the name is actually Richland Lutheran Cemetery, as can be seen by the sign directly at the entrance. The cemetery is fairly small in size and is surrounded by a wooded area of trees. We had gathered our information on the computer as to where this cemetery was, so we weren't positive we had found the right place or not. We also saw a small bridge on the same road, just a ways down from the cemetery. We were expecting a rather large bridge and instead found a very small one that didn't appear to have any water beneath it at all. The bridge doesn't seem much like a bridge at all these days and if there was a big drop under the bridge before, it is no longer there today. If I were to classify it, I wouldn't even call it a bridge. It's more like a section of the road with a rail on each side of the dirt. We assumed that perhaps the land had changed over time, or we had the wrong bridge entirely.

Just to be sure we had the right cemetery, we drove quite a ways in both directions on Dice Road to make sure there weren't any other cemeteries on the road and finally came back to the one we originally stopped at. We stayed a while, taking photos and doing some EVP work. The cemetery felt peaceful for the most part. As I walked towards the middle of the cemetery where most of the older stones seemed to be, I felt a temperature change and asked Sandra to walk the same path as I had, to see if she noticed it. Then we asked Bill to come over with the laser thermometer to take some readings. The temperature was essentially the same all over in that area; I dismissed what I had felt. Because the cemetery is surrounded by trees, it's in a bit of a valley and that could explain the slight difference in the temperature towards the middle of the land.

We stayed until it was dark, waiting to see the woman in white 'float' across the cemetery, as reported by various local people. We never saw her while we were there. With our photos, we captured a few orbs, but nothing more than that and nothing that couldn't be explained away by logical deductions. We captured one strange sound on audio that sounds similar to a seagull or another type of bird. Since we were surrounded by the forest area, I pretty much dismissed this EVP because it could have been some type of bird. Sandra and I had been experimenting with a pendulum that night, during the time I picked up the EVP on my digital recorder, but I am not sure if there is a connection between the two or not. All in all, this cemetery felt very peaceful and tranquil, and we didn't experience anything out of the ordinary. Perhaps the spirits were quiet that night? Maybe the woman didn't want to show herself to us, or maybe the legend surrounding this cemetery is just that—a legend.

PINE RIDGE CEMETERY, BAY CITY

Pine Ridge Cemetery was opened in 1858 after James Birney gave the land at the corner of Trumble and Columbus for use as a cemetery so his brother, George, could be buried there. James Birney was a circuit judge as well as a senator in Michigan and was involved in much of the growth that took place in Bay City during its early years. The only cemetery in the town at the time was Potters Field, and it contained the bodies of the first pioneers of Bay City. When Pine Ridge Cemetery was opened, they closed the old Potters Field cemetery. This excerpt was taken from the Bay City Daily Journal dated December 14, 1871.

> "On the site of the old graveyard on 12th Street between Washington and Saginaw Streets may yet be seen scattered graves with headstones mixed in with the house erected last summer."

Pine Ridge Cemetery remained privately owned, and over time, it had become an abandoned cemetery, which in turn meant a neglected cemetery. In 2000, a non-profit group called Friends of the Pine Ridge was formed, and they have been working on restoring abandoned Pine Ridge Cemetery and cleaning up years of neglect. James Birney himself is now buried in the cemetery, along with over 154 Civil War veterans.

Pine Ridge has a section dedicated to the Civil War soldiers who are buried there, and a cannon was also placed in this section along with a memorial sign to honor them. Because of the rich history of this cemetery and the amount of older gravestones within it, I wanted to investigate there—not because of claims of ghostly activity, but out of sheer curiosity.

The cemetery sits right in the city, with houses and businesses surrounding it. There is also another cemetery which borders it on one side. At the time, we didn't know what this cemetery was, but I later found out that it is Seaman's Cemetery, named

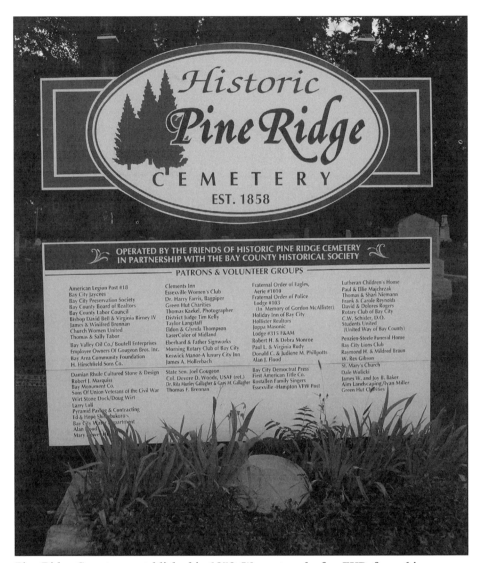

Pine Ridge Cemetery, established in 1858. We captured a few EVPs from this cemetery which is located right in downtown Bay City.

after George D. Seaman, who platted it. You can no longer tell where the one cemetery ends and the other begins, due to overgrowth and weeds in many places. We walked around this historical cemetery, looking at the many gravestones which from neglect were either tipped over, broken, or completely missing. Even with the obvious neglect in some areas, though, you can see that it is being slowly restored by the Friends of the Pine Ridge. They are to be commended for undertaking such a task.

The cemetery had a peaceful feeling and some of the older markers are really amazing to look at. We spent some time in the section dedicated to the Civil War veterans, doing some EVP work with our recorders, and of course taking photographs. Sandra and I had spent quite some time in the back corner of the cemetery near the adjacent burial grounds taking pictures. During this time, I kept seeing strange shapes in my photos and we were trying to figure out what they were. We later discovered they were simply bugs, as it was warm outside at the time. We captured an EVP during this time when I was telling Sandra about an orb that I saw in one of my pictures that seemed pretty large. As I am talking you can hear a man talking over top of me as I speak. He seems to be saying,

"There's a fish."

Sounds a bit strange considering we were not discussing fish at all. The EVP is not a first class EVP, which means it's open to some interpretation as to what it says. (Please visit www. ghostprism.com.)

We captured two other EVPs from our trip to this cemetery, and one of them presents some great evidence in the theory that ghosts and spirits can interact with us, proving that they aren't just leftover residual energy. As we walked through the cemetery when we first got there, it was still daylight. I came upon a very large tree that had something hanging from the leaves. They were long and skinny objects, and as I got closer I wondered what kind of tree I was looking at because I had never seen anything like it before. I asked Sandra and Bill to look at the tree, and during the time, I captured this EVP. I was saying to Sandra and Bill that the objects looked like beans. The voice I captured on audio says (after I make my comment),

"Yeah."

The Native American Catawba tree (aka bean tree) that is located in Pine Ridge Cemetery. I was asking Bill and Sandra what type of tree this was when we captured an EVP.

It sounds like a female voice to me and she is speaking softly, but loud enough so you can hear what she is saying. Being quite curious as to what the tree was, I found out from a search that the tree is an Indian bean tree which has heart-shaped leaves and very long pods that resemble green beans in shape, but much longer. The beans hanging off the tree in this cemetery were a foot long or more.

The third EVP we walked away with was taken in the Civil War section of the cemetery. Bill and I spent a few minutes walking around, looking at the names and dates on some of the gravestones in this area. It was fairly quiet at the time as we wandered about, and getting a bit darker. The EVP we caught from this section is a male who whispers,

"Yes."

I am not sure who he was talking to, if anyone. I know Bill and I weren't talking to each other at the time, so I don't believe he was interacting with us.

One spot in the back of the cemetery and off towards the side seemed a bit creepy. There is an old shed that sits there—probably a storage shed. There was some graffiti on the side of the shed (more specifically, a pentagram), and the shed sat near a bunch of overgrown weeds and flowers. Scattered in between the tall weeds and flowers were headstones that were broken or tipped over, so that played a part in how that particular area felt in general. Sometimes, your mind can play tricks on you according to what your eyes are taking in.

In contrast to this area, the rest of the cemetery felt peaceful, other than the sounds of traffic going by because it is so close to businesses and houses. Although we didn't get any overwhelming evidence in our photos, we were able to get enough EVPs from this cemetery to lead us to believe there are definitely spirits there. The cemetery is so rich with the city's history that it creates just the perfect combination to make it interesting enough to visit again. If you want to see for yourself if the spirits of the city's founders and Civil War soldiers roam this cemetery, pay Pine Ridge Cemetery a visit.

ST. JOSEPH CATHOLIC CEMETERY

While doing research, I stumbled upon an old newspaper article from the *Bay City Times* in 1951 with the headline *"Forgotten City of the Dead."* This immediately caught my attention and so I continued to read. The story was about the abandoned St. Joseph Catholic cemetery near the Visitation church that stands nearby, and how there was some uncertainty as to who owned it or who was in charge of it. In 1905, it was published that the Catholic cemetery board was in charge of it, but the cemetery eventually became an abandoned one and the church itself didn't have names or

dates on record of the people who were buried there. The story in 1951 mentioned that old broken stones could still be found on the spot where the old cemetery once was, and some of the stones were large enough to be able to read the transcriptions on them. The article also stated that, "No parish in Bay City lays claim to it."

In another article in the *Bay City Times*, roughly a week after the first one, apparently the mystery had been solved. It was discovered that some of the families of those buried at the location had given the land to the church for the cemetery. In 1951, city officials had discussed the possibility of putting a playground in the spot were the old cemetery used to be.

Since I just recently came upon these old articles about this cemetery, I am not sure whether a playground was erected on this piece of land or not, but if it was, I surely hope that it was made sure that the remaining bodies were recovered and buried in another local cemetery. It was common practice, back in the day, for many cities to move bodies about as if it wasn't a big deal. To me, once a person is buried in a particular spot, they should remain there without being disturbed. Although I don't have the belief that spirits of people remain attached to where they are buried, I can certainly understand why any spirit would be upset if their body was being moved all over town.

Cases of hauntings where bodies were moved seem to create some upset at times with the spirits of those people involved. The movie *Poltergeist* is one example showing what I am referring to, though presented in a theatrical style. What is more upsetting to me is that there are countless abandoned cemeteries all over the United States that for whatever reason go from one year to the next, with nobody caring about those buried there. The Native Americans who once lived in Bay City consider their burial mounds sacred ground. Why aren't *other* cemeteries treated as such?

The land where the old St. Joseph Cemetery sat could in fact carry the restless spirits of those pioneers who were forgotten so long ago. It would definitely be interesting to find out if any of the spirits are upset over what happened there. The author of the first article said it all with the headline, "Forgotten City of the Dead." It seems that Bay City had quite a few cemeteries that saw the same fate as this one did. Some bodies were moved, others were left where they were laid, but were built over top of with houses or businesses. This to me is a practice that shouldn't happen in Bay City, or anywhere else.

I believe the Visitation church mentioned here might be Our Lady of the Visitation Church, which is rumored to be haunted by a bloody hand that appears in the church. Of course, that is just another Bay City urban legend. Or is it?

6

MISCELLANEOUS HAUNTINGS

When I began to write my outline for this book, I wanted to divide the ghost stories up into chapters according to where and what type they were. Buildings, cemeteries, Native American legends, etc. Some stories cannot be classified into any of these chapters, so I decided to have this chapter, so I could highlight some shorter stories which would not fit into the other categories.

Because Bay City is so rich in history and includes stories like Paul Bunyan, the underground railroad, the lumberjack days, Hell's Half Mile and more—there are plenty of stories to go along with its history. It's quite a fascinating city when you think of the history that is attached to it. I myself love reading about the history of old buildings, especially when we are doing investigations at older buildings. The spirits seem to speak out from within the walls of the buildings, telling you their stories as they whisper in your ear. There are urban legends and ghostly tales from cities across the country, and as curious humans, we seek to know the real truth. In this book, I have tried to share not only the urban legends and ghost stories, but to also share any findings that myself and my team have found while trying to investigate— so we could make our own decision about the rumors of hauntings.

Hells' Half Mile was said to be so haunted by past spirits, especially those of the Sauk Indians, that some people wouldn't step foot in the city at all. While doing the research, I came across tidbits here and there about stories that were vague, or I didn't have enough access to be able to search the stories further. You may have heard some of these stories before, and I am sure you might hear them again, but perhaps each time you do, you will learn something new that you didn't know before.

DELTA COLLEGE

Delta College sits midway between the cities of Bay City, Midland, and Saginaw. There is also the Delta College Planetarium which is on Center Street in Bay City, near Wenonah Park. The site where the planetarium now sits is where the old Wenonah Hotel used to be, until it caught fire in 1977. Interestingly enough, the Wenonah Hotel was built in 1908, two years after the old Fraser Hotel caught fire. Although I haven't heard any stories of the planetarium being haunted, rumors abound about Delta college being haunted. People report hearing footsteps in the building along with seeing apparitions roam the halls at the facility.

The college was at the top of my list of places to investigate because of the rumor that apparitions had been seen. Delta College advises that these hauntings are just rumors and none of the staff or current students have reported any paranormal activity within the building. So where do these rumors begin? Oftentimes, there's a sliver of truth. I, for one, will be keeping my eye out for an opportunity to find out first hand.

JB MEINBERG PUB

The JB Meinberg pub is located on Hamilton Avenue in Saginaw. The pub is said to be haunted by an old bar maid who has been seen checking on tables in the back section of the bar, and even whispering in the customers' ears, asking them if they want a drink. It is also rumored that she has been seen walking around in the hall of the old pub. I've been told that each year a story is featured about this haunted pub during Halloween in the local paper in Saginaw. If you are in the Saginaw area and happen to be thirsty, perhaps you should stop at JB Meinberg's to see if the old bar maid takes your drink order.

MIDLAND CINEMAS

Midland Cinemas in Midland supposedly sits on some land that was used by farmers at one time. As the story goes, six people died on the land during the time it was used for farming, and now the Midland Cinemas are said to be haunted. Do those who died on the land still roam there? Some employees have reported that the stories of the hauntings are true. Ex-employees have said that the night cleaners and people working the projection booth know that the tales are indeed factual. One employee was doing some night cleaning and heard what sounded like a woman's screams coming from one of the projection areas—she seemed to be screaming for help. He also heard what sounded like nails being scratched on the door as if she were trying to get out of the room. Because the door locks from the outside of the booth and he himself had locked it before he heard the woman screaming, he became frightened and ran out, never to do night cleaning at the cinemas again. Strange noises and apparitions have also been seen sitting in the seats when the cinemas aren't open, late at night.

SAGINAW RIVER LIGHT

The Saginaw River Light is also known as the Saginaw River Range Lighthouse. It was built in 1876, and is now owned by the Dow Chemical Company. The Saginaw River Marine Historical Society is working with Dow on restoring the lighthouse from its current state and it is not open to the public right now.

In 1998, Troy Taylor, author of over fifty-two books on ghosts and ghost hunting, wrote an article about the Saginaw River

Light. He has given me permission to reprint part of the article here to share with you.

"Ghosts and old lighthouses often seem to go together. Many lighthouses have ghosts, or at least tales of ghosts, that usually revolve around lonely lighthouse keepers or shipwrecks caused by some failure to keep the tower light burning. The commonly haunted spot in an old lighthouse is invariably the stairs to the tower....why? Those who are familiar with a "residual" haunting will say that the energy expended on those stairs has left an imprint that repeats itself over and over again causing the sound of phantom footsteps to be heard. When the human occupants of the lighthouse try to track down a source for the sounds...there is usually no one there. There are also those other lighthouses....haunted by phantoms from the past that still reach out to the present day. The tower of Michigan's old Saginaw River Light is said to be a place where a ghost of the past may walk....or at least it sounds as if he does. This lighthouse is said to be haunted, but no one really knows who the ghost might be. Many believe that it could be the spirit of an old lighthouse keeper who died in the building. Before passing on, he begged his family to keep the light going and to never let it go out. By all accounts, the family did just that and the light was kept burning for many years.

Shortly after the Coast Guard took over the light, strange things started to be reported here. Namely it was the sound of heavy boots on the iron staircase that were often heard. When the men would go to check and see who was on the stairs, they would find no one there. Another haunted spot is the Presque Isle Light near Alpena, Michigan. The tale is told here of a lighthouse keeper's wife who went insane because of the loneliness of her husband's position. It is said that he imprisoned the madwoman in a cell below the lighthouse and she spent her last days there, shrieking insanely. It is said that her screams can still be heard today."

—Troy Taylor
Haunted Michigan, Haunted Lighthouses

Along with stories of haunted Michigan lighthouses, there are chilling tales of haunted ghost ships that once traveled through the Great Lakes. Some of these tales include actual sightings of phantom ships that perished in the waters, one even being due to an actual ghost on board. Perhaps these stories are just fabricated legends told to others to make them wonder, or maybe there is some truth to the stories that haunted lighthouses and ghost ships are real.

7

UNDERSTANDING GHOSTS

I am going to depart for a bit from sharing more stories about haunted locations so that I can touch briefly on the actual ghosts themselves. What is the actual definition of a ghost? Why do you think they haunt a specific location? Do ghosts only appear to some people while not appearing to others? These are questions that are commonly asked when talking about ghosts and haunted locations. Hopefully, we can sort through some of the theories and talk a bit about why ghosts appear in the first place and what their reason is for showing up.

The actual definition of a ghost can vary slightly from person to person, but the basic definition of a ghost is a disembodied spirit who is earthbound and cannot 'move on' or 'cross over' into the spirit world. Some people care to use spirit and ghost interchangeably, and in essence, they are both spirits, so this is not entirely incorrect. The difference though, lies in the theory that spirits have in fact crossed over, while ghosts have not crossed over, for whatever reason that may be. Within the definition of what a ghost is, lies definitions for numerous types of ghosts that can cause even further confusion and reasons for discussion about how they operate and what they are doing here. Some of the definitions within the category of ghost themselves follow, so you can understand a bit more about what you might encounter in any haunted location.

INTERACTIVE GHOSTS

Interactive ghosts are spirits who have not crossed over and might be 'stuck' here for various reasons. I prefer not to think that they are stuck here, but I have no evidence that they may not be stuck, so I use the term because it's a widely-known expression that most people have heard before. They might be attached to a house that they once lived in, or have unfinished business that they need to attend to.

The theory about spirits having unfinished business is a common one, especially when one person in a house or building seems to have more paranormal experiences than others in the same location. The spirit might be trying to send a message to one particular person for a reason—a common theory is that they are seeking this communication to help heal their own issues, or help heal the person they are trying to communicate with. Such a case might be a father who died and is now trying to communicate with his son, who he had a troubled relationship with. Perhaps the son lives in the father's old house, or lives in a house that doesn't connect with the father directly. In either case, the father would like to say something to his son to heal the relationship in some manner, so he sticks close to the son, trying his best to talk to him.

Another reason that an interactive ghost might be hanging around is that a person might be directly attracting the ghost, or ghosts. Most times this is done unknowingly by the person involved, but it could also be a case of someone thinking that communicating with ghosts is all fun and games and shouldn't be taken seriously—which it should. Sensitives and psychics can also become 'spirit magnets' because they are able to see, hear, or feel the spirits. The spirits are aware of this, and because they want someone to notice them, they become drawn to these psychic people so they can interact with them.

In other cases, people who see ghost hunters on popular ghost hunting shows recording spirit voices want to try it out themselves, and they find themselves in trouble down the road when a spirit or ghost is drawn to them, thinking the person really wants to communicate with them. Yes, this really happens! People who are grieving over a loved-one's passing can get caught up with trying to record their loved one on tape so they can communicate with them.

Last year, I received a call from a woman who believed she was hearing her son on a cassette recorder that she would use in her home. She was very stricken with grief over the passing of her son the year before, and was wrapped up in her sorrow surrounding his death. She called me in a panic after hearing another voice on the recorder whom she didn't think was her son's, and wanted some help from me. I talked with her on the phone several times, trying to tell her about the dangers of trying to communicate this way with her son. Perhaps she *was* communicating with her son, but she was also opening the door for other spirits to come through. It's almost like holding up a sign and saying, "I am here, come talk to me." The danger with this is that, unless you have the knowledge that you need to deal with ghosts and hauntings, you may get what you ask for—but it might not be the spirit you were trying to communicate with. Instead, you might drag in a negative spirit who you certainly wouldn't want hanging around your house. The other danger with doing this, especially if you are grieving a loss, is that it can really hurt someone on an emotional level. It's best that the person go and talk to someone professionally to deal with the loss and begin the healing process.

Interactive ghosts are the most common and they are the ones most notorious for turning lights on and off, and messing with objects and other things that you might encounter at a haunted location. There are many types of interactive ghosts, ranging from a passed-over loved one, to a negative spirit who doesn't want to leave, to a child ghost who might simply be lost. There are so many different types of interactive spirits that it would be rather lengthy to go into each and every one of them. I will discuss a few more types of ghosts so you can get the general idea and then we can move on.

POLTERGEISTS—
NOISY GHOSTS OR JUST ENERGY?

Poltergeists have been regarded as the 'noisy ghosts' (German translation). They are the ones who make a fuss by stomping around, banging objects, opening and closing doors and cabinets, and throwing objects off a table or off a wall, such as a picture. Poltergeists have the reputation for being angry ghosts, or just plain mischievous ghosts who want to wreak havoc on a person or place. Those people who have experienced poltergeist activity can attest to the fact that it is not a fun experience, and can turn a house upside down with negative antics by the time it's done. While this might be true, there is one other theory that has come to light recently that might explain this type of activity.

The new theory that has surfaced fairly recently is that poltergeist activity might in fact be directly connected to a pre-adolescent female who, because of her hormonal state being in a huge change, is affecting her surroundings with her energy via telekinesis (the ability to move objects with the power of the mind). This same phenomenon can occur with someone who is in a high state of anxiety or nervousness, altering the energy around them and actually moving objects and making noises themselves. Most times this is done on a subconscious level and without them being aware of it, so they are afraid and worried that they have a poltergeist in their house, when in fact, they are creating the activity themselves. The most common theory is the one surrounding young females, because in many cases the activity seems to stop when the female isn't home, or it follows her to the next house if the family moves. This theory is still being explored, but I think it is a good one because everything is energy and there is still a lot that can be learned about how energy works and is intertwined with our thoughts and emotional state.

The mind-body-spirit connection is now being looked at by doctors who are realizing that our thoughts play a huge role in our physical health and in our lives. In the case of poltergeist activity, I think this is something that needs to be investigated even further because the findings might really be astounding.

Residual Hauntings

In the case of residual hauntings and ghosts, the ghost is not actually there—and this is another example of how energy can affect our surroundings, even years down the road. In some cases, hundreds of years later.

It's thought that residual hauntings are a n imprint of something that has occurred in the past, and the most common event involved in this scenario is a tragic event. For example, Gettysburg in Pennsylvania is known for having residual hauntings. Apparitions of men on horses and in battle are common sightings at this battle site, by ghost hunters and non-ghost hunters alike. The thought here is that when seeing these apparitions, you aren't actually seeing an interactive ghost who can communicate with you, but an imprint of the energy that has been left over from the event itself. Since some people who study quantum physics and energy might tell you that all time is *now*, meaning there is no past, present, or future, this theory might make sense. Sometimes, past, present, and future events might cross lines and the energy could be intertwined, essentially all happening at once. That is a lot to wrap your mind around when you think about it, but I don't think it is a possibility that should be ignored.

Common activity that might be experienced when you have a residual haunting can range anywhere from hearing footsteps to seeing apparitions. One common occurrence when hearing footsteps or noises is that this would occur at the same time each day, perhaps the time when someone died or at the moment of a tragic event that led to their demise. If you hear footsteps at 9 pm each night in the same location of your house or in a building, it might be a good idea to explore residual hauntings more.

NEGATIVE GHOSTS

Negative ghosts are just that, negative ghosts. Why are they so negative? Well, it's my personal belief that we carry our personality from this life over to the next one, so if someone was negative or nasty when they were alive, that person would be that way after crossing over. Some people believe that once you cross over, you are healed and have all of the answers, therefore, that negative would no longer exist. But I am not so sure that this theory is true, and I still believe that we hold onto our personalities, quirks, beliefs, and thought-patterns when we die. If someone had mental problems when they were alive, or they were a serial killer, murderer, or had some other psychological problem when they were living, did they die an angry person? Before they died did they suddenly heal those emotions that tormented them when they were alive? Yes, this is possible I suppose, but some people could carry much of that with them when crossing over, creating the negative ghost.

Negative ghosts can be responsible for things similar to poltergeist activity, and much of what is being done is being done because of anger and their need to take their feelings out on other people—much like when they were alive. They might throw things, make loud noises, move things around in the home, taunt the people living in the house, try to frighten them, and much more.

I also hold the belief that energy is drawn to similar energy, so if you are a negative person in general, or even depressed, you might attract the same energy towards yourself, including negative ghosts. Negative ghosts want to draw off of that negative energy, making themselves more powerful and giving themselves more energy to wreak havoc on the living. It's a good idea when dealing with a negative ghost not to give them anger back or remain in a negative state. Screaming and swearing at them might only make matters worse in the long run. You can try to tell them to get out with an assertive tone of voice, but try not to be aggressive, because that might just upset them even more than they already are—which wouldn't be a good thing.

Sometimes negative ghosts just need some talking to from someone who seems to care about them, or maybe they are lonely and want some attention. Other times, negative ghosts can be very stubborn and just want to play games with someone's mind for the heck of it. It all depends on their personality and why they are finding joy in upsetting someone in their own home, or place of business.

A negative ghost could haunt a historical building as well, and the possibilities are endless for why they are choosing a particular location for their antics. They might have a connection to the location, or they might not. There are no experts in this field and so there are no concrete answers to why ghosts do what they do, only theories that can be shared.

Non-Human Entities

Non-human entities by definition are not ghosts of people who once lived on earth, but non-human entities who have never lived an earthly life. Non-human entities can include angels, spirit beings, negative entities, and demons. The non-human entities I will speak about here are the demons, only because I don't feel I should leave them out for the sake of defining ghost activity more clearly, even though they are not considered to be ghosts at all. Angels and spirit guides do not usually disturb people, as they are here to help us and not harm us.

Demons are thought to be the opposite of angels, and are considered by many as fallen angels. Those angels who have fallen from grace and now live on the dark side and 'not in the light.' Demons and negative entities are in another category altogether and there is much debate about whether they exist or not. If you go by the Bible and are a religious person, you might be more likely to believe in demons and negative entities. The movie "*The Exorcist*" is one-of-a-kind and I believe one of the first of its kind to bring demonic activity to the forefront of society. Up until then, it was something that wasn't talked about much in most circles. With the changing times and the continued rise of paranormal groups, it's more commonly talked about these

days. In the paranormal community, there are large debates about whether demons actually exist, much like other topics we discuss between those who study these things.

My personal opinion is that belief in demons is strongly connected to religious beliefs, as are many other paranormal-related beliefs. That, coupled with our own individual experiences, leads each person to make a decision about what to believe in. Whether you believe in demons or not, if you are trying to help someone who does believe they have demonic activity in their home or place of business, it's something you have to read about and learn about so you can try to help them the best way possible.

Demonic hauntings are the nastiest of hauntings, and include many scenarios for what you might experience. When dealing with a demonic haunting, you are dealing with an entity who is not only smart, but can mask itself into various shapes, forms, and even voices. They can mask themselves as any object or person and try to trick you into believing their lies. This of course is theory just as anything else, and I have not personally dealt with a demonic haunting to this day. I have to say that I am thankful that I haven't. I have, however, dealt with negative spirits, but I don't feel that they were negative entities, which can be pretty nasty compared to a negative spirit. Entities in my mind, have much more power than simply a negative spirit, so you are dealing with a whole different range of problems.

As mentioned above, the movie "*The Exorcist*" was about demons, but not a demonic haunting. The movie was about the demonic possession of a young girl who was possessed by a demon, or demons. Whether or not demons and demonic possessions can take place are personal for each who believes or does not believe. Many Catholics believe in possession and the Catholic church is the one most referenced when speaking about exorcisms, largely because the Catholic church has used priests when dealing with exorcisms and the movie brought that fact to the forefront. Other religious beliefs might support exorcisms, but I am only familiar with the Catholic church when it comes to conducting exorcisms.

The biggest problem when dealing with a possession case involves figuring out whether the person is mentally stable and without psychological problems before carrying forward with more help like an exorcism. There seem to be quite a few people these days who call themselves experts on demonology, but I would recommend to anyone that they first consult their local church to which they belong (if they belong to one) and a psychiatric doctor for help. If you cannot find help there, then you can turn to paranormal investigators, and hopefully, they can point you in the right direction. Getting references for assistance with demonic hauntings is imperative, because you need help from people who have experience with such things and who will know how to deal with them.

Demonic hauntings will be the subject of many discussions and debates for many years, as will spirits and ghosts and a wide range of other paranormal phenomena. Everyone comes to their own decision based upon how they have grown up, their environment, and their personal experiences over the years. Sometimes it's hard to believe in something that you have not personally experienced, and that is understandable. Other times, you base your opinion on books that you have read, stories told to you, and people you meet who have experienced such things.

I personally have the belief that the world was created with balance, and has to remain in balance to keep revolving, and evolving. Where there is good, there is bad. Where there is light, there is dark. How could you know one without the other? Whether that dark world includes actual demons, I cannot say. I can, however, base my opinion on what I have experienced and my religious beliefs, and I will say that I do believe that there are at least negative entities out there who have inflicted pain and suffering on people in various ways.

I have gone over a few examples of types of ghosts, but have not even scratched the surface on the whole subject .There are so many new theories out there today about them that I would have to write another book to include them all here. But I did want to go over them briefly before discussing interactions with ghosts and spirits, what you can do, what you shouldn't do, and what the best ways are to capture evidence when doing paranormal investigations.

Spirits Are People, Too

I wrote an article for the PRISM website titled "*Spirits Are People Too.*" I wrote it after I listened to an Internet radio show in which they had been discussing Ouija boards and if they were harmful to use, or if they were just in fact a game that could be used without serious consequences. I felt my thoughts would add another dimension to those presented on the show. They compared the use of Ouija boards to audio recorders that investigators use to capture spirit voices on audio recordings, saying that taking audio recordings is similar to using the Ouija board. My experience has shown me that this may not be the case.

I have been a paranormal investigator for a few years. I go out and help people in their homes who believe they have ghostly activity taking place, or who are unsure and want some answers to what is going on. I have been studying actual spirits for quite some time now though—roughly 17 years. I have read books about them: what they are made of, what types of spirits are out there, why they are here, etc. I have spoken to other people about spirits and have run across some great teachers along the way who have shared stories with me and taught me things about spirits that I never knew, or even dreamed I would know. I have written articles about animal guides and totems (animal spirit guides), spirit guides, and self-help articles for people who are searching for something that they know is there, but cannot seem to find. I have a sincere reverence for all things living, and all spirits who have crossed over. I have had spirit communications both in my sleep, and while being in the awake state. I have done spirit communications for people, helping them to gain some closure on the death of a loved one, and helping them heal from within. I do not label myself as a spirit medium, but I do have the ability, just as all people do. Many people think that it is a special gift that only some are privy to, but I disagree with that, and believe that each and every person has the capability to communicate with spirits on a telepathic, psychic level. We are all energy and all made up from the same 'stuff.' Whether we are alive or dead does not make a difference. We are all *people*.

I also have a sincere reverence for the Native American culture and ways, especially their strong connection to nature and their respect for spirits in general. This is something that has helped me immensely when dealing with things of a spiritual and paranormal nature, and I believe that it helps me to answer questions from people who are trying to understand spirits and ghosts.

Having said all that, I want to begin to share with you my views on spirits and how we should try to interact with them, without upsetting them in any way. I also want to go over some methods that can be used during paranormal investigations that don't involve the act of provoking the spirits so evidence can be gained, and why I feel that science isn't the key to unlocking the doors of the paranormal world. I will replace the word ghost with the word spirit in this part of the book because this information relates to all spirits, not just ghosts. I personally don't care for the word ghost because it immediately seems to get a negative or fearful reaction from people when you say it. The information I am going to share isn't based on scientific evidence, but some of this knowledge has been gained from researching and using various methods while out with my team on investigations.

SCIENCE ISN'T THE ONLY WAY

Within the paranormal community, the word science is thrown around *a lot*. Hundreds of paranormal groups form each year and it seems like the 'in' thing to list on a mission statement for these

groups is using scientific methods to investigate the paranormal. I find some problems with this statement, perhaps because I studied spirits from a spiritual perspective for so long, and continue to do so even now. The word spiritual is often mistaken with the word religious, but they are not the same and the meanings are certainly not the same. Some groups feel that the only way to investigate is with scientific methods, but I feel that the methods being used cannot really be considered scientific to begin with. The spirit world isn't about science, it's about energy and matters of the heart. It's about those things that you cannot see or touch most of the time, but you can definitely feel.

The use of technology for investigations is common, and I would rather use the word technology than the word science because it seems to be a more accurate word for what is being done. When you conduct a scientific experiment, there are certain methods being used, and they are normally carried out in a controlled environment so that the test results will be accurate. Investigators cannot control the environment on each case, because each case is different. Each location is different, as well—each location would have a different temperature, a different humidity reading, different people involved, and different backgrounds. This is certainly not a controlled environment by any means. Exact methods can be used when using the equipment, but there are even doubts about the equipment being used and whether or not it can really document paranormal activity if it were to occur.

EMF (electro magnetic field) detectors are pieces of equipment used to pick up electro magnetic fields, and many investigators believe that a spike in the electromagnetic field detector might indicate the presence of a ghost. But there are so many electrical fields while investigating that come from natural sources, I don't feel that EMF detectors are as useful as some people may think they are. It's true that if there is no other explanation for a spike on an EMF detector, and you happen to get a photo or an EVP at the same time, then that might indicate spirit activity, but I am still undecided as to how big a role an EMF detector should play in investigations.

I often hear people say, 'one day we will prove that ghosts exist' with science. I am not sure that this will ever happen. If people are non-believers in the paranormal, showing them scientific evidence isn't going to change their minds. However, a personal experience will. And I can bet that their personal experience won't have a thing to do with science at all. Science can be useful, don't get me wrong here. Science might be supportive when it comes to analyzing the frequency of a spirit's voice, or for inventing new equipment that can be utilized by the investigator, but I think that is where it ends. Technology plays a big part in investigations with most groups, but I don't think it is necessary to have the best or most expensive equipment out there. I think that common sense and respect go a lot further than any EMF detector will.

THE USE OF PSYCHICS

Along with the people who feel that science is the only way, comes the thought that psychics shouldn't be used for investigations. I believe that a balance should be kept between using technology and psychics, and both methods should be utilized. Psychics who can communicate with spirits have one foot in the spirit world, and any good psychic knows, for the most part, how the spirits and spirit world operates. If you use the information that a psychic gives to you at a particular location and you can back up that information with a validation about names, dates, etc., why shouldn't it be considered evidence? Even if you don't get a validation about a name, I don't think that they should be disqualified immediately. Not all locations have the availability of every name of every person whose ever stepped foot in the building. It is nice to have that validation, but I don't feel it's totally necessary, especially when you are dealing with a haunting in a home. Validation might be nice for data or record keeping, but it won't do any good for a person living in fear and anxiety because they think they are in danger from a ghost or ghosts.

After a psychic that our group used was no longer in the group, I wondered if I should try to find another one to replace them. A few of my investigators thought that it would be best not to have one at all, feeling that the psychic takes too much time away from the actual investigation with equipment. But I said, "When someone calls me and is in fear about who or what is in their house, there are two things that they say to me. One: Who is it? and Two: "Get it out of my house." If we are not psychics who are capable of telling them who it is in their home and we don't know how to get it out, what good will we be to them? My viewpoint is that my job is to help the homeowner, no matter what it takes. I will not disqualify the use of a psychic for my own benefit, or just to prove that ghosts exist or don't exist by scientific means. My job is to help the people who are living in fear in their own homes, and if that means we have to utilize the abilities of a psychic, I will do it. This isn't about me and what I want or need, it's about what our clients need.

Why Are Ghosts Here?

I touched on this topic a little when I went over the types of ghosts that are believed to exist, but I want to go into this a bit more so that I can talk about it from a more spiritual point of view. I feel that ghosts are here most of the time to get attention. I am not talking about getting attention the way a child would want to get a parent's attention, but about getting some attention from another person, just as we all like to have it from other people while we are interacting with them. If you walk into a room full of people and nobody acknowledges the fact that you have just walked into the room, how do you feel? Do you feel as if you are being ignored by everyone there? Do you wonder if they are mad at you or don't like you for some reason? I think this is what the spirits go through when they are probably waving their hands at us saying, "Look, I am over here! Don't you see me?" Whether they are in a house that they use to live in, an old building, or a place they use to work, when they see us, they want us to *acknowledge* them. They want us to have conversations with them, ask them questions about how they are, why they are here, what they want. And when that doesn't happen, they might get a bit upset or frustrated and try very hard to get our attention.

When I get calls from people wanting help and I ask them what types of activity they have had in their homes, two of the most common answers are objects moving or making noise, and banging noises. I think these answers are common because when the spirits are trying to talk to someone and that person doesn't acknowledge them or answer them, they try their best to make their presence known, in whatever way they can. So they bang things around and move objects, realizing the person will stand up and take notice to what is going on around them. They figure, "Hey, this is working; they are noticing that I moved their keys around and they are wondering what the heck is going on. Eventually, they will figure out that I am trying to talk to them and that they are ignoring me!"

For those spirits that are here because they feel they have unfinished business or they want to speak with a particular person, the activity can be much worse. They might slam doors very loudly, flash the lights on and off, or throw things. Of course, this might just be the antics of a mischievous spirit, but I feel that in the majority of the cases, it's just a spirit who wants you to notice them. Spirits are just people without physical bodies, plain and simple. I think that sometimes people fail to really think about this and remember it when they are dealing with spirits. If we keep this in the back of our minds when dealing with a spirit, things might go much smoother.

USE RESPECT AT ALL TIMES

When working with spirits on any level, you want to make sure that you respect them as you would any other person whom you meet or come in contact with on a daily basis. Remember that a spirit is just a person who no longer has a physical body.

Using respect when dealing with spirits is a good practice to have, whether you are a seasoned paranormal investigator or just curious about them in general.

Some people have the view that provoking the spirits will enable them to capture some fantastic evidence, but this isn't the best method available for getting some great evidence that the spirit world indeed exists. And it may not be the most effective, either, especially because it can generate results that could endanger you or others around you. I hold the belief that because spirits are people without bodies, they still have emotions and feelings, even though they have passed over and do not live in the physical world anymore as we do. Provoking them can bring negative reactions from them due to the fact that they have been treated with disrespect.

So, with that said, never provoke a spirit or ghost using harsh language or nasty attitudes, because they might retaliate in a negative fashion that could cause some major problems all around. Some of the consequences that can result from taunting or provoking spirits include, but are not limited to: negative reactions from the ghost resulting in thrown objects at things or people, harmful energy that results in after-effects leftover in the house or building, and physical discomfort or actual bodily harm to the person showing disrespect or to others who are present at the time. Provoking could leave behind serious issues left for the homeowner or building owner to deal with, and we certainly do not want that to happen when the reason we are there to begin with is to help them with the paranormal activity.

If you use non-threatening methods for gaining evidence that ghosts exist, you can still walk away with great results and feel good about yourself, knowing that no harm has come to the ghosts or anyone else present during the process. If you are curious about ghosts or want to capture some fantastic evidence, try to develop a rapport with them and treat them with respect and dignity. You might find that it makes a big difference in the amount of evidence that you can collect, and it will enhance your research even further because once spirits know that you have a genuine interest in their well-being. Because of this, they will be more forthcoming in their communications with you as a whole.

USING HONEY
TO COMMUNICATE WITH SPIRITS

So how does one use that *honey* to interact and communicate with spirits, ultimately capturing evidence that you can be proud of? I will tell you a bit about the things that I have learned while doing investigations that seem to help out quite a bit. My standpoint has always been that I don't do investigations to capture phenomenal evidence. In fact, that is not my goal at all. My goal is to help out our clients any way that I can. I am not doing this to prove anything to anyone because I think each person needs to come to their own conclusion about spirits and that will happen when it should happen. I do, however, like the thought of being able to share an EVP with someone and say, "Listen to this; it is amazing!" I would share any piece of evidence that the team got—of course I would. But I am not doing this just for the sake of getting evidence to prove anything. With that said, I have to say that I go into any investigation (me *and* my team do) from a spiritual perspective. I know that I am essentially the same as the spirit I am trying to talk to. The only difference between us is the fact that I have a physical body. So when I talk to them, I use respect at all times and will never ever provoke a spirit.

When I first began doing investigations, EVPs terrified me. I was afraid to hear the words "get out" or "leave now" being screamed at me in a growling voice. But now, EVPs have become my passion during any investigation. I love the fact that an audio recorder enables me to hear the spirit speak to me, even if it is later that night or the next day, since I don't hear most of my recordings when I am recording them. My team and I have quite a few amazing EVPs that we have captured during investigations and I have become known, at times, as the EVP expert on the team. (Please visit www.ghostprism.com.) Because spirits are on a higher vibration then we are, we don't hear them when they are speaking to us. We would have to raise our vibration (like many psychic mediums do) or they would have to lower their vibration, coming down to our level of frequency. Because most people don't know how to raise their vibration to hear them, audio recorders are a blessing when it comes to hearing a spirit speaking to us.

Because my team and I do not use provocation to capture evidence, each spirit voice on tape that we have recorded has come from the fact that we have talked to the spirits in a respectful manner. I believe that this method works, because we have some of the best EVPs I have heard (and I am not just saying this because it's my group). We have some of the most amazing communications from spirits and some people have wondered if they were actually spirits talking and not us talking. I always tell them to listen to the pitch and tone of the voice speaking, and if they listen close enough, they can tell the difference between a spirit and us. During our investigations at one local building (which I will highlight later in the book), we have done some research when it comes to recording spirits. We have done experiments with different recording methods and kept track of when we seem to get the most EVPs when we are investigating.

The thing that seems to be constant for us is the fact that we get more EVPs when most of the group is in one spot, in a group of three or more people. This could be due to the fact that our energy is more centered, being in one spot, as opposed to being scattered throughout the building. The spirits would have more energy to work with coming from this one place, so it would be easier for them to utilize it. Another theory is that when we are in a group, we are having more conversations with each other. The spirits like to join our conversations, no matter what the topic might be. We also capture more EVP evidence when we are talking then when we are being silent and using the question method, asking spirits specific questions and hoping they answer us. One thing that always remains the same is that we are genuinely concerned for the spirit's welfare and we reflect this in the way that we talk to them.

THINGS TO REMEMBER DURING INVESTIGATIONS

Attitude Makes a Difference

One of my friends was on an unofficial investigation with a friend of hers in a popular haunted location a few years ago. She commented to me after she got back that this person seemed to have a real negative attitude when they were there and it was very apparent to her during the time they were investigating. Afterwards, when they both reviewed their evidence, she found out that she captured more spirit voices on tape than her friend did. I feel that the reason the other person didn't get as many spirit voices on tape was because there was a negative frame of mind when the investigation was taking place.

I think that this also plays a huge part in the response you get back from spirits. Why would a spirit want to talk to someone who is in such a negative and nasty mood? I know I don't like being around negative people, so this makes perfect sense to me. Now, you might say that perhaps she just had better luck that night than her friend did. Could be, but I am not convinced of that. With occasions such as this one, you have to remember to put some basic psychology and spiritual principles to use, instead of just thinking about the methods and technology. Everyone immediately thinks about the scientific aspect of it, but most people don't factor in the things that you can't equate to science—the attitude that you carry when you walk into a location, the feelings that you have towards the spirits, and the respect that you use when you are dealing with them. Remember that you are dealing with people, not just things. They are not to be toyed with and deserve the utmost respect from anyone who is trying to communicate with them in any way. Forget for a second about your evidence to remember that they are just like you are.

Psychology Can Be Helpful

I believe that psychology plays a huge role in this field. Whether you are researching the aspects of spirits and spirit interaction and communication, or dealing with clients who are fearful and confused, psychology is something that needs to be studied. I am not suggesting that you go out and sign yourself up at the nearest college to be a psychologist, but I am suggesting that you speak with people who have psychology degrees, read up on human interactions and the human thought process, as well as psychology relating to spirits. There are a few people in this field who are more knowledgeable than others when it comes to parapsychology. Lloyd Auerbach holds a MS in parapsychology from JFK University, is an accomplished author, professor, and lecturer, and knows quite a bit about psychology as it relates to spirits and paranormal investigations. He is a wealth of information and has done extensive research in the parapsychology field. He says interesting things about humans and whether our consciousness survives once we pass over from this life on earth. Although it has not been proven that our consciousness does survive, it's a prominent theory that it does. Lloyd has written amazing books on parapsychology, ghost hunting, and other topics of interest. He also shares quite a few articles on his website that you can browse through at www.mindreader.com. I highly recommend Lloyd's books and articles to anyone who is involved with paranormal investigations.

When a client contacts you for help, there are many factors that can come into play. The client's upbringing, their religious beliefs, their mental and emotional state of mind, and a host of other things. Make sure that you deal with each client with compassion, but at the same time, you'll want to look at things objectively and not jump to any conclusions. Try to understand where the client is coming from in terms of how they feel. Many clients don't care about the evidence you might collect in their house, they just want someone to talk to about how they feel, or they want someone to rid their home of any unwelcome guests. Sometimes, I think that we all should have a degree in psychology before ever stepping foot into someone's house for an investigation. I know this is not practical or possible, so reading about the subjects of psychology and parapsychology are the next best thing. If you know someone in either field, talk to them. Ask questions, listen to interviews done by people such as Lloyd, and broaden your thought process to include the human side of ghost hunting. I cannot say strongly enough how much of a help this can be to both you and your team when dealing with clients and cases.

Much of the perspective here is geared towards the paranormal investigator, but if you are a homeowner who feels you have ghostly activity in your home, most of the same suggestions on dealing with spirits apply. If you are at the beginning stages of just finding out there is a ghost or ghosts in your home, try not to assume that the ghost is trying to harm you or your family members, because 99 percent of the time, they just want to communicate with other people. If you are curious as to why they are there, you can ask them questions. They know when you are honestly asking and want an actual response from them, and they will know when you are not truly trying to find out more about them.

If you at any time, feel threatened by activity from ghosts in your house, you can try to talk to them using some forcefulness, just as long as you don't sound too aggressive. When you don't know what you are dealing with, it is always better to remain on the side of caution and take things slowly, until you have a better understanding of the circumstances that surround the goings-on in your house. Each ghost is different, and they all have different reasons as to why they are hanging around. Each person is also different, so depending on how much you already know about spirits and ghosts, determine the course of action to take. At any rate, you don't want to upset a ghost who could already be negative in nature, so it's best to use some of the suggestions that I have talked about in regards to what paranormal investigators use. It's better safe than sorry, especially where your family is concerned.

9

HISTORICAL HAUNTS OUTSIDE THE TRI-CITIES AREA

The tri-cities area of Bay City, Midland, and Saginaw have some amazing stories about haunted houses, cemeteries, and buildings, but if you would like to take a day's drive and check out some other haunted cities in Michigan, I am going to include a few historical buildings in this chapter. They are fairly well-known haunted locations near my town, and anyone who likes to go ghost hunting in this area is familiar with the buildings. All of the buildings I will be showcasing are public buildings that are open to the public on a daily basis. Two of them, at one time, were hotels and are now restaurants, and one is an opera house, which today houses pubic events and even rents out the first-floor space for wedding receptions, graduations, and other occasions. If you get a chance to drive out to any of these locations you won't be sorry. The history behind each one is fascinating, and the ghost stories that go along with them are fabulous.

THE HOLLY HOTEL

THE HISTORY

Listed on the United States Register of Historic Places, the Holly Hotel is referred to by many as one of the most haunted historic buildings in Michigan. In 1908, the first proprietor of the hotel, John Hirst, opened the Hirst Hotel for business, on the land where the old Washington House once stood. In the early 1900s, at least twenty-five trains would pass through Holly on a daily basis, bringing freight, local passengers, and transients who would frequent local saloons that could be found on Broad and Martha Streets. There were many brawls and free-for-alls that took place in the area of Martha Street. After an 1880 incident between a traveling circus group and some local rowdy men that sent most of the fighters to jail and the others to the hospital, Martha Street earned the new name of "Battle Alley" by the local people. The name is still referenced today and there is a historical marker which tells about the tale of Battle Alley and a local "saloon smasher" named Carry Nation was brought in at the request of a local prohibition committee to settle down the town. She used her umbrella as a weapon as she walked through the local saloons talking to the rowdy men about 'demon rum' and its sins. Battle Alley became the first paved road in village in 1910.

In 1913, the Hirst Hotel caught fire and the second and third floors were destroyed. Then, in 1912, Joseph P. Allen bought the hotel and re-named it the Holly Inn. One year later, another fire almost destroyed the hotel again, and afterwards, Joseph Allen remodeled both the outside and inside of the hotel. The inside was fashioned using a Queen Anne Victorian design, and fine linens and food were always used at the hotel. This attracted visitors from all over the United States, and the hotel quickly became the center for village activity.

As technology grew and the trains no longer ran through Holly as they once use to, the decline of the quaint shops and hotels in the city began, and the hotel was no exception, becoming a boarding house and pizza place in the 1970s. On January 19, 1978, at the exact hour and date of the first fire that had taken place in 1913, the hotel once again caught fire. This time the damage was so great that it was considered to be demolished, but in 1978 a two-year restoration of the building was underway, and it was being restored with great detail back to its former splendor.

The Ghosts

Over the years, both guests and employees alike have reported ghostly activity in the hotel. It is no longer used as a hotel, but as a restaurant where they serve people daily and have various events throughout the year. Reports of smelling cigar smoke are common when no logical reason for the smell can be found, and the smell of a flowery-type perfume is commonly mentioned also. The cigar smoke is believed to be that of John Hirst, the previous owner of the hotel when it was called the Hirst Hotel. It's believed that Mr. Hirst has not passed on due to the fire that destroyed the hotel in 1913, ending his ownership of the hotel. Mr. Hirst's ghost seems to be the ghost that manifests most frequently at the hotel, but actual apparitions of him are said to be rare. If you smell cigar smoke at the hotel, you might be in the presence of Mr. Hirst, as this is how he presents himself most of the time. He does not seem to be very happy with the renovations that have gone on in the hotel either, and might believe that he is still the man in charge.

Nora Kane is the reported to be the spirit responsible for the smell of the flowery perfume that people talk about. She is said to show up in the back hallway and main bar most often, as that is where the smell of her perfume lingers the most. Historical documents state that Nora loved music, and still enjoys playing the piano, even now. She shows up frequently in photos that are taken at the hotel, especially wedding photos. If you think you may have encountered Nora at the hotel in apparition form, you can view her picture in the lobby for verification as to what she looks like. Nora also likes to sing and can be heard throughout some of the different dining rooms in the hotel late at night. If you are near the piano, she might even whisper in your ear and ask you to play a song for her.

The most active ghost at the hotel seems to be that of a little girl between the ages of nine to thirteen. She favors the kitchen the most and is also believed to be the ghost who runs back and forth on the stairways. In the kitchen, she has an affinity for the meat clever (of all things!), teapots, and some other cooking utensils that are in the kitchen. It should be noted that many of the cooking utensils and china are turn-of-the-century objects, and wouldn't be unfamiliar to a child of that era.

The little girl who loves the kitchen is believed to be either a young girl who may have died after a stable accident nearby, or the daughter of Nora Kane, the spirit who brings in the smell of flowers to the hotel on a regular basis with her perfume. In the early 1990s, a séance was conducted in the hotel and the spirit of this little girl reportedly made her presence known to those at that event.

If you are ever in Holly, you'll need to pay a visit to the Holly Hotel, and maybe you can experience the perfume that is believed to be Nora's, or smell the cigar smoke of the former owner, John, who seems to be overseeing the hotel's business even after his death. And if you happen to feel something brush across your leg while you are there, that might be Leona, John's dog, who might love the old hotel just as much as his owner does.

THE FENTON HOTEL TAVERN & GRILLE

A GHOST WHO JUST WANTS HIS JACK DANIELS

The Fenton Hotel Tavern & Grille, formerly named just the Fenton Hotel, has been featured in the books *"Weird Michigan"* by Linda S. Godfrey, and *"Haunted Michigan"* by Gerald S. Hunter. As I said previously, these ghostly hotels are well known in this area of Michigan, if not all of the state.

The Fenton Hotel resides in the small town of Fenton, Michigan, between Ann Arbor and Lansing, right off U.S. 23 heading north towards Flint. The hotel was built in 1856 and has a historical marker just as the Holly Hotel does. The hotel changed owners quite a few times, with its current owners being Nick and Peggy Sorise. The Fenton Hotel Tavern & Grille celebrated it's 150th year in 2006, and Nick and Peggy decided to do some renovations, including adding on "tavern & grille" to its former name of Fenton Hotel.

The hotel staff and customers have experienced quite a few ghostly encounters with deceased spirits who still roam the place—everyone from an old custodian named Emery to a rather promiscuous ghost who likes to grope the waitresses by grabbing their arms or buttocks. Emery's old room upstairs is still there, and people seem to think that they have heard him walking the second floor and pounding on walls after the last customers have left the building. The second floor is also home to the old ballroom with its tiled floors, and men's and women's bathrooms, but it is no longer in use today for access to the public.

One of the most interesting cases of haunting activity at the hotel is a man who sits at Table 32 and orders a Jack Daniels shot on the rocks from the bartender. When the drink is poured and is ready to be served, the man is nowhere to be found, and definitely not at Table 32. This has been a recurring event at the hotel and I assume that the apparition of the ghost must be a fairly solid one if he is actually getting them to pour a drink for him! Unfortunately, he disappears before he can have his drink, so perhaps he just takes pleasure in messing around with the bartenders a bit, or he could be part of a residual type of haunting if he appears at the same time and same day of the week. It would be interesting to find out more about the mysterious man who orders his shot of Jack Daniels on a regular basis. Oh what stories I am sure he could tell!

The hotel is still active today, especially the bar area, where glasses have flown out of their designated hanging spots out into the room, only to come crashing down on something or someone. Reports of a black cat being seen walking across the floor by some waitresses coupled with the groping ghost who likes to get frisky with them, would definitely make this an interesting place to work each day. Another supernatural story includes the third stall in the women's bathroom where women have complained that someone who they could not see pulled their hair. There's a theory that this particular ghost might be that of an old prostitute who use to serve her clients on the third floor and became pregnant, causing her to hang herself in the hotel.

In the book, "*Weird Michigan*," they reported their own ghostly encounter at the hotel when they paid a visit to the hotel. They were given a tour of the second and third floors, the floors that most people never see while in the hotel. As they were walking around upstairs, one of them said that they heard a woman whisper in their ear. When they were finished with the tour, they noticed some wax on one of the cameras which had not previously been there. They said there wasn't a candle at the table they were sitting at downstairs, and they didn't see any candles upstairs that were lit for any wax to have dripped onto the camera. Maybe they were joined by some of the resident ghosts that day as they walked the second and third floors. Emery the old custodian might have been walking with them to make sure that they didn't harm the building in any way, or maybe another ghost just wanted some company and joined them, candle in hand, so they could light the way for the guests.

THE PERFORMING GHOSTS

In the smaller community of Howell in Livingston County, Michigan, sits a gem-in-the-rough called the Opera House, which stands proudly in the middle of the Historic district of town at the corner of Grand River and Walnut Street. The Opera House is run by the Livingston Arts Council, a non-profit organization dedicated to bring art to the community and restoring the Opera House to its original glory. Living twenty-five minutes away from Howell in Pickney, I had never heard of the Opera House. I never really had a reason to travel to Howell, although I had been through it a few times. Almost two years after setting foot in this beautiful building, I am now a regular volunteer at the Opera House spending many hours when I can, and I like to help out with giving tours of the upstairs portion of the building. I think it is a worthwhile cause that will be well-worth the effort when it is all said and done.

My group and I have been investigating at the Opera House since the fall of 2006 and we have extensive compiled reports. It has become one of our favorite places to investigate—not because of the spirits that inhabit the building, but because of the building itself. It has a tendency to draw you in, almost calling out your name. Once you are inside, it will captivate your senses with its architectural design of the upstairs, a place that had been sitting silent for over thirty years, like a time capsule. Because it is my favorite place, I have saved it for last. I have quite a bit to say about this treasure and I hope that each one of you will take a trip one day to visit this fabulous building. I know the spirits there will be glad that you came!

The Opera House as it stands today, in the Historic District in Howell, Michigan.

THE HISTORY

The original building was 20' x 40' in size, and was the first public building in Howell. It was called the Eagle Tavern, and became the "center of population for all business matters of the pioneer settlement." They held religious services at the Eagle Tavern as well. In 1837, a log barn was built onto the tavern so there would be a spot for the horses and other things to be contained. Samuel Waddell was injured during the construction of the barn and died from his injuries. This was noted as the first death in the township. The first fire in the village to do severe damage was September 28, 1857, and swept through the Eagle Hotel and almost the entire line of buildings on the south side of Grand River.

The Opera House was built in 1881, costing $11,000 dollars and was built with a seating capacity of 1,000 people. Up until the 1930s, when the upper portion stopped production on stage events, the Opera House was used as the community center for the town. Many events took place there, including school classes, graduations, political speeches, and the activities of a court house (before the court house down the street was built). After the upstairs portion of the building stopped having productions on the stage, it was mainly used for storage for the hardware store that was in business on the first floor of the building.

The upstairs portion of the building remained sealed off until the year 2000, when the Livingston Arts Council (L.A.C.) bought the building and began plans for renovation to use the building as a community gathering place where art was the main focus. It is nothing less than amazing that the second floor of the building is still in its original state, frozen in time from the day it was closed off. Some of the original structures that can be seen upstairs are the original gas flame chandelier which hangs in the center of the ceiling, the original ticket booth door where people would purchase 10, 20, and 30 cent tickets for the shows, and the 3 rows of benches on each side of the balcony where the show-goers would sit and watch the entertainment. Lead glass windows adorn the upstairs, and all but two of them still have the original lead glass, although the L.A.C has plans to replace the windows soon.

Looking at the stage, the original backdrop still hangs from the ceiling and has not been unrolled for over forty years. The actors and actresses would have the flickering amber glow from the oil-burning footlights held in tin reflectors at the edge of the stage shine on their faces as they performed for their audience during each show. In 1910, the Opera House had its first non-gas lighting on the stage, and well-known people such as Ty Cobb and Henry Ford, have stood on the Opera House stage, along with some who are not so well-known, like Jessie Bonstelle, who is the namesake of the Bonstelle Theater in Detroit, Michigan. Jessie Bonstelle was an actress who also started several theater companies, working closely with E.D. Stair, newspaper mogul and one-time manager of the Opera House. Together they launched several successful road shows and made quite a nice profit doing so.

The stage at the Opera House, complete with the original backdrop and trap door, where the actors would sneak down to the dressing room during performances.

The original backdrop, which hasn't been unrolled in over thirty years.

When first doing research on the Opera House, I discovered quite a bit of historical information on both the land and the building itself, including the buildings that stood on the land before the Opera House was there. Once a tavern and later a hotel, the Opera House has had many inhabitants throughout its history, and many community events that went along with it. Besides the school affairs, court house functions, and even a post office, many local secret society groups met in the building, including the Goodfellows and the Masons, just to name a few. Adding to the mystery that often surrounds such secret societies, is another mystery about the tunnels that ran under the Opera House, to the other side of the street. There is speculation as to what they were used for, but nobody knows for sure. The tunnels are now closed off, but you can see the remnants of where they used to be when you stand downstairs in the basement of the Opera House today.

Today, the L.A.C. is still working on renovations of the Opera House. A first-floor renovation was finished in May of 2007, and their goal now is to raise funds for the major renovation of the second floor. Since its renovation, the first-floor is being rented out to anyone who wishes to hold an event at the location. After the renovations, my group and I decided it was the perfect place to hold a paranormal expo (June 2008). The mixture of the history of the building, its charm and the spirits, was the perfect place for our gathering. The Opera House is also host to the L.A.C.'s continuous art events such as art shows, craft fairs, fund raising for other non-profit groups, and musical events like the new Acoustic Cafe' and local bands who perform on the first floor. Until the second floor restoration is complete, the L.A.C. will continue to hold its events on the first floor, raising the money to restore the grandeur of the second floor.

The first tour I had of the building was back in 2006, during Howell's popular Melon Festival. This was before the first-floor renovation had even taken place, and the condition of the downstairs at the time was a bit rough, but nevertheless, it was still beautiful. As the tour continued on and we traveled upstairs, I was in awe again at how the building seemed so frozen in time. I could almost imagine how the building came to life when the people traveled up the once-grand staircase in the front of the building to see the performance for that night. Women and men dressed in their finest and ready for a night of theatrical happenings, gathered in this gorgeous building to see the show. If only the Opera House walls could talk.

Or do they?

THE GHOST STORIES

When I took the tour of the Opera House led by Lindsay Root, Opera House Historian, I was told about the building's resident ghost, Meredith, who resides on one of the back staircases near the ticket booth room. This staircase is lovingly referred to as the 'haunted staircase' when tours are given to the public. The story of Meredith is a love story, one filled with sadness because she witnessed her husband in the balcony many years ago with another woman. Two psychics on two different occasions (who did not know each other), told some of the L.A.C. staff that Meredith roamed up and down the staircase, still upset over her husband's infidelity. Meredith has become a much-talked-about ghost during public tours at the Opera House, adding excitement in the eyes of those who hear her sad story. People are always given the choice to take the haunted or non-haunted staircase when walking up to the balcony area. Many brave souls decide to take the haunted staircase!

Other initial reports that were given to me included little children who have been seen in the balcony area. This could be related to the fact that so many young children were there many years ago being schooled in the Opera House when classes were held there. With so many activities being held there over the years, there have been thousands of children through the building, so the fact that apparitions of children are being seen would make perfect sense.

When I first asked about paranormal activity at the Opera House, I didn't hear stories about anything flying off the walls, loud noises, or mischievous types of activity. Everyone who I encountered that spent any length of time at the Opera House didn't seem to mind the fact that there might be some ghosts lurking about the building, so I pretty much knew that the activity couldn't be anything threatening or 'over-the-top.' After investigating this building for close to two years, I think I know why that is. But I will share my thoughts about this later in the story.

The haunted staircase that leads up to the balcony. It is believed that one upset ghost named Meredith roams up and down the stairs.

Sharon Fisher, sales manager and past vice president of the L.A.C. has had quite a few personal experiences at the Opera House and does in fact believe that there are spirits in the building, saying, "I do not have any idea who these spirits are, but I feel they are somehow tied to the Opera House through their own life experiences. I feel they are familiar with things that are going on, and that they like them. I think that if they didn't, we would see or experience something negative from them." Even though Sharon doesn't feel there are negative spirits at the Opera House, there are a few occasions when she has been a bit spooked by something she has heard or seen. On one occasion, Sharon was on the first floor when she heard a loud noise coming from upstairs that seemed to be something being dragged across the floor. It started from one wall and the dragging continued across one third of the floor space. It happened three times with about five minute intervals between each incident.

One a separate occasion in the fall of 2007, Sharon was downstairs setting up the room for a rental the next day. She was placing tablecloths on the round tables, and when she turned in the direction of a table across the room which she had already placed a tablecloth on, she saw that one tablecloth was moving, as if someone was holding onto a portion of the linen with two fingers. The cloth continued to slide across the table with a triangular shape at the top where the fingers would be, and then finally slid completely off the table and dropped to the floor in a perfect fashion. Sharon said even after it was on the floor, it stayed in a cone shape, just at it had been when it was moving. After witnessing this phenomena, she asked herself, "Did I just see what I thought I saw?" answering herself with a, "Yes, I just saw what I thought I saw."

Sharon, like Lindsay Root, Opera House Historian, gives tours of the upstairs so that people can see the beauty of the old Opera House and appreciate its historical value. On one such tour, she was talking to the tour-goers in the balcony when one of the stately large doors on the second floor below them slammed so loud that Sharon thought it would fall off its hinges. Nobody was downstairs below them at the time and the sound effect certainly added something unique to Sharon's tour that day.

She had another experience with the same door in the fall of 2007 on one of the weekends when the L.A.C. was cleaning up the basement and bringing some items up to the second floor to store them in the room where the ticket booth was located. There are two sets of large double doors that lead from the main room to the area near the ticket booth where the grand staircase use to be. Because the doors are heavier and swing open, when they are working on clean-up or during tours, they will prop one or both of the doors open. Sometimes, they will prop one of the doors open with an extension cord from one of the lights that are plugged in, running the cord under the door so it is jammed in tight enough for the door to stay open. They will also prop the doors open with heavy objects to keep them open while they are walking back and forth between them. Sharon was carrying one of the boxes from the basement into the ticket booth room, and when she walked through the set of doors closest to the ticket booth, the door that was propped open with a heavy object slammed shut behind her. Sharon didn't think much of it at the time, thinking that perhaps she bumped it and it closed behind her. But when she went through the door again, she knew that wasn't the case. As she walked back through the doors again, the door with the extension cord slammed shut as well. Sharon knows that when the extension cord is jammed under the door, nothing will move it. Well…almost nothing!

Because Sharon is in the building so much by herself, she has had many personal experiences relating to the spirits that other L.A.C. staff haven't had. She has also heard stories from visitors to the Opera House who have told her their experiences. Visitors who haven't witnessed any phenomena are always curious about paranormal activity in the building and will ask Sharon about it when they are taking a tour. Sharon will tell them what she knows, and she says they will ask a lot of questions. "I usually end the conversation with 'believe what you want' and everyone is comfortable with that, drawing their own conclusions." Sharon hopes that the Opera

The ticket booth door, where patrons by the hundreds would step up and pay to see shows at the Opera House.

From the stage looking out, you can see the balcony, as well as the two sets of old double doors that lead back into the gathering area where the patrons would come up the grand staircase.

House "will be restored to its Victorian beauty and the entire complex will become the art and cultural center for all communities in Livingston County."

OUR INVESTIGATIONS

Because my group has done so many investigations at the Opera House, have so many reports, and have done so much research, I am going to try to highlight some of what we have experienced. I cannot possibly list all of the spirit voices that we have picked up on tape from here, so I will showcase some of my favorites. You can, of course go, to our website (www. ghostprism.com) and hear the majority of the audio that we have obtained from the Opera House, along with some photos that we have taken there as well.

I plan on continuing our study into this building and am always curious if the activity will change over time, according to what is going on in the building. That is part of the research that we have been conducting here and will continue to do as long as possible. Even while writing this book, more incidents, which could be deemed paranormal, are popping up, and this seems to be increasing as time goes by. Perhaps the ghosts are excited that I am talking about them in the book—you never know.

As with any investigation that we do, historical research is very important to us and we always try to research any location that we are investigating. I personally think that it is imperative and helps us to make better determinations as to what is occurring and whether it is paranormal in nature or not. I share anything that I find with the L.A.C. staff, just in case they might not have knowledge of something that I have found. (There is a historian on the L.A.C. staff who regularly researches the Opera House as well.)

Inside the Opera House, you will find old playbills, tickets, photos of some of the people who used to perform on the stage, and other historical artifacts. They are kept inside glass cases on the second floor, so if you ever pay them a visit, make sure to stop and browse through these wonderful antiques. On more than one occasion, we have found playbills and other old items while digging around upstairs under the old seats. The historian is usually with us and is as curious as we are as to what we can find while rummaging around beneath the old dusty bench seats. It is indeed a treasure when we do find something.

Guests to the Opera House have also found items by accident, like a younger girl who looked down into one of the smaller holes in the floor upstairs and found a coin from the 1800s. Her find that day managed to make it into the local paper and we still tell the story to people taking the tours—even now.

OUR FIRST INVESTIGATION

Our first investigation was September 16, 2006. There were seven P.R.I.S.M members in attendance, along with Lindsay

Root, the Opera House historian. Because the building has an open structure, it isn't particularly easy to do investigations there. The original first-floor area was very open before the restoration took place, with one large main room, the Walnut Room (a smaller area in the back), and another small area that was a connecting room to the Walnut Room and near the bathroom. Next to the bathroom was a storage room which used to be a part of the old barn that was added on many years ago. At one time, the old barn beams were very visible on the ceiling in this room. The room is still in use today, even after the restoration, and is still being used as a storage area. The upstairs second floor and balcony is a very open space, and sound can be heard from every direction when standing up there because there aren't any rooms to block off the sound from one to the next.

I decided to split the team up to investigate, and we took turns between the first and second floors, and basement. I had to decide whether to have any of us in the balcony area when people were below on the main second-floor area—and decided that I would. At this time in my paranormal research, I was beginning to experiment with EVP sessions and whether total quiet with only a question and answer forum should be used. From my research at the Opera House alone, I know now that my initial way was not the best way to conduct EVP sessions. Some people disagree with my thinking, and also believe that you should only conduct EVP sessions with, at the most, two people present. Because of the fact that energy plays a part in the way spirits communicate with us, I think it is actually beneficial to have more than two people present while trying to capture EVPs; this way, the spirits have more energy to work with, and more conversation to join in on.

EVP EVIDENCE

During this investigation, we had a psychic on board, and she reported that she was picking up numerous spirits in the building. One spirit that she immediately mentioned on the

A rare photo of some of the actors and actresses who would perform on the Opera House stage in the late 1800's and 1900's.

first floor was a man who was a regular visitor when the tavern was on the grounds. She said that she could see him spitting his tobacco into an old spittoon, also known as a cuspidor. They were receptacles made for tobacco chewers to spit in and were found in public buildings, such as the old tavern. She didn't pick up his name during this particular investigation, but in subsequent investigations she said he was known as "Old Jack." She said Old Jack was still there, hanging around the bar and spitting in the spittoon. During one of our later investigations, after she had mentioned Old Jack, Sandra and Bill decided to try to make contact with him to see if he would talk to them. Sandra asked Old Jack if he was there, and the reply on her recorder was, "Yes." This was one occasion when asking a direct question of a spirit actually paid off with a direct answer. Unfortunately, her further questions didn't receive answers from Old Jack.

The tavern that Jack would have been hanging out in would be the Eagle Tavern, built in 1835. I haven't been able to find out much about people who actually frequented the old tavern, though. Also, without a last name for Jack, it would be difficult to verify who he was, but he himself verified that he was there with his *yes* response to Sandra.

During our initial investigation here, we didn't experience anything in the way of moving objects, slamming doors, footsteps, or other amazing phenomena, but a couple team members had some problems with their cameras and video equipment shutting off on them. Both the video camera being used and a few digital cameras spontaneously shut off to the right of the ticket booth room, very close to the haunted staircase. While we cannot say for sure whether this was paranormal in nature or not, it happened to more than one person and more than once during our investigation. Four of the team members also felt cold spots in the same area where the cameras were shutting off, so that could be a connection that indicates some spirit activity.

We walked away with seven EVPs from our first investigation, and one of them is by far our most incredible EVP to date. (Please visit www.ghostprism.com.) It's a class A EVP, which means that this is the EVP most investigators strive for, since it is clearly audible—even without using headphones. Class A EVPs are also so clear to everyone listening, that there are no debates as to what is being said by the spirit. This EVP was captured on my faithful old cassette recorder and was so clear that I did not have to edit it in any way.

The psychic we had with us this night was leaving with another team member. There were four of us standing on the second floor, and I was standing at a table right below the stage area. The psychic walked up to me to say goodbye and give me a hug, and as she did, a woman clearly said,

"Bye, thank you."

The woman's voice sounds so amazing that people have asked if it was one of us speaking and not a spirit, but I assure everyone that none of us said this and we were pretty shocked when we heard the EVP. It is truly remarkable, and to this day, I am still in awe at how clear she sounds. If you listen close enough to the EVP, you can tell that this is a spirit simply from the pitch of her voice while she is talking. Because spirits are on a higher vibration, sometimes this is something that can be picked up when they are communicating with us. I do believe that they actually communicate with us telepathically, and aren't actually standing with their mouths hanging over our microphones as we have our recordings running. I believe that most spirit communication is done telepathically, much like how a spirit medium would connect with those from the other side.

Although not a Class A EVP, we also captured a Class B EVP (an EVP that can be agreed upon as to what is being said, but softer sounding, and sometimes in a whisper) during this investigation that is pretty fascinating. I captured this particular spirit voice while I was sitting in the balcony with my recorder. I was sitting on one of the benches quietly, listening for any unusual sounds and watching for anything that might catch my eye. I agree with Grant Wilson, one of the investigators from the television show *Ghost Hunters* who says that it is a good idea to just sit in a room and get the feel of it and your surroundings.

This is what I was doing on the balcony bench that night when I captured a very sad EVP of a man's voice.

As I played back my recorder the next day, I heard a man whisper,

"I love her."

It is a bone-chilling sound to me, not because I think it is threatening in any way, but because of the sadness I can hear coming from the man's voice as he declares his love. The EVP is softer, but can still be heard, and he seems to be in pain as he sighs when he says he loves her—almost a declaration that he loves her, but he cannot be with her. I am not sure who the man is or who he was talking about, but it is one of my favorite spirit communications that I have heard so far from those we have taken from the Opera House.

Our first investigation did not provide much evidence in the way of photos or video footage. There is quite a bit of dust floating around the second floor of the building, and the first floor also had more dust at this time, before the renovations. Dust naturally leads to the topic of orbs in photos. My position on orbs is that many of them are dust particles or objects caused from lens reflection or other camera malfunctions. I also cannot say whether an orb is a spirit or not, because there is just no way to prove it, plain and simple. I have the belief that when looking at a photo for orbs, a true orb will be by itself or with only a few other orbs, and not just reflections and such. The orb must omit its own light and look three-dimensional, and it must be solid in color as opposed to something more transparent. Orbs are debated about between paranormal enthusiasts and I must say that I lean towards the fact that most of them are just dust or something else, but sometimes we run across a few photos that we have taken with some nice orbs in them that we do highlight on our website to share with other people.

We did, however, take a ton of pictures the first time and we did catch orbs, caused mostly from dust particles. There are also a lot of ropes and hanging light bulbs upstairs, so that can be an obstacle when taking photos. The chandelier in the middle of the upstairs ceiling would cause reflections in our pictures, so it was a bit of a challenge at times to get some good photos. Even without substantial proof from cameras or video, we did capture quite a few EVPs and everyone loved the building and had a great time.

OUR SECOND INVESTIGATION

Our second investigation was just a month later, on October 7th. This time there were a few more investigators present, as my team was growing back then, so we were well staffed that night to try to go in and do more research on the building. We experienced a cold spot on the second floor that seemed to hover for quite some time. Four of us felt this cold spot in the middle of the room, so Bill checked the temperature with the temperature meter, which didn't show a noticeable difference. All of us could still feel the cold spot in one area, but not around it. The windows were not open and we couldn't find a draft to explain where this chilly air would have been coming from. One of us took a photo while we were investigating the cold spot and the photo did display an orb in the area as we were trying to debunk the cold feeling. It makes for an interesting night.

More EVPs were captured on our second investigation—six total, which was pretty close to the number from the first investigation. I had taken the previous recordings and put them on a disc so that I could play them back for everybody while we were there. As I was playing one of the previous recordings, the psychic asked, "Who is that?" (What she was actually hearing was her own voice.) The psychic didn't recognize her voice; being new to listening to this kind of evidence, this sometimes happens. As I was playing back the previous recordings, I also had my cassette recorder taping us. I like to turn them on as soon as we enter each investigation, even as we are setting up. During the time she was asking me who she was hearing, I captured an EVP. The EVP sounds like a man and he said, "do do do doty." Within five minutes time, he said it again, same

A shot taken from the
balcony looking down
towards the stage.
You can see the dust
particles in this photo
that are often mistaken
for actual orbs.

words, exactly the same way. While normally I might consider this to be evidence of a residual haunting, this time I knew that it was in fact an active spirit. The reason? The word *doty* connects to the person who was asking me the question. He answered her by telling her, it was her. His voice seems to have a sarcastic sound to it, as if to say, "Don't you know what you sound like?!" Quite interesting indeed.

Two things really fascinate me about this particular EVP. The first is, he said it twice within a certain time frame, and said the exact same thing both times. This means that not only is this an active spirit, but one that was paying full attention to our conversation as we went about our business that night. Perhaps because nobody responded to him the first time, he felt the need to repeat himself again for a second time? Maybe he was just so sarcastic that he wanted to say it a second time for the heck of it; I am not sure. The second thing that really stands out to me about this recording is that from what he said, I can assume that spirits know things about us without us having to offer information.

One time I was watching a television show where an investigator had captured an EVP of her first name. She told the interviewer that the spirit must have known her name from the name badge she had on. I thought this was humorous when she said it, and even now I chuckle at it. I somewhat knew back then, that spirits don't need name badges or signs or introductions for them to know who we are—they just know. How do they know? That I cannot say for sure, but because I have a belief that the spirit world is a place of amazing knowledge and infinite wisdom, it just makes sense to me that spirits wouldn't need to see something to know it. They would know our first names, last names, and other information about us that we, of course, do not know about them. Does it make you uncomfortable to hear this? It can be a bit unsettling at times when you really think about it, but it doesn't really bother me, because I don't fear the spirits, especially the Opera House spirits.

Another EVP that was captured that night was from my recorder, and it again speaks volumes about what spirits know about us. I was sitting up in the balcony with two other investigators and we were talking about the building, and how 'homey' it felt to be in it. We were quietly chit-chatting with each other and sat up in the balcony for at least a half hour or more. That night, my eye happened to be very irritated, so the next day when reviewing my tape, I laid on the couch with a washcloth on my eyelid, which was now swollen. As I laid there with my eyes closed, suddenly I heard a man whisper my name! I almost fell off the couch when I heard "Lisa" being whispered in my ear. This EVP occurred during the time we had sat in the balcony talking. I knew it wasn't the male investigator talking with us because it was not his voice, and he wouldn't whisper to me anyway, because I tell all of my investigators NOT to whisper during investigations, just so we can make sure that we don't make a mistake during a recording and think that one of us is a spirit.

I must say that hearing my name whispered by a spirit was a very freaky thing. He didn't say anything other than my name, so was he talking to me or about someone else? Again, the burden lies in the proof. The strange thing about this voice is that it sounded pretty close to the male voice who had whispered, "I love her." The team joked around and said that maybe I was the one that he loved. Possible? I suppose so. Probable? Who knows? Anything *is* possible.

THIRD INVESTIGATION

On November 18, 2006 we headed back to the Opera House for our third investigation. There were nine P.R.I.S.M members present plus Lindsay Root. On this particular occasion, we did a séance in the basement, per our psychic's request. Her feeling was that there were some spirits there who needed to speak with us, and she felt a séance might help. Although this is not a usual practice, I was curious as to what might happen. We conducted the séance in the basement, and everyone was present at the time. Some of us were sitting at the table with the psychic, while the others were standing around the table watching, taking photos, and recording audio. While nothing incredibly out of the ordinary happened during the séance, we ended up with fifteen audio recordings that night of spirits, with most of them captured in the basement either before, during, or after we conducted the séance. This did seem different from our other investigations because we had only captured a few EVPs from the basement on our previous times there. This led me to believe that either the séance brought about the amount of EVPs that night, or it was the fact that all of us were in the same area for a longer period of time—something that hadn't happened before.

During the set-up for the séance, we ended up with a few recordings of people singing or humming. During the psychic's closing prayer, after the séance, a woman seemed to whisper, "yes," in agreement with the prayer. We also heard some laughing on our recorders, and a few "hi" EVPs as well. The séance went well with no negative effects, so we were pleased with the results.

I honestly cannot say why we captured so many EVPs that night, but I think it might have been due to the amount of energy that was created with all of us in such a localized spot for that length of time. We were also specifically trying to speak with them via the séance, so that may have played a part in it as well. The spirits at the Opera House really do like when they are getting attention from other people.

Aside from the spirit voices that we caught on tape, there were a few personal experiences that some of the investigators had while we were there. Two investigators were standing just below the stage and they both witnessed what seemed to be a light streak zipping by on the stage. I asked them if it could have been a reflection from outside, such as car lights from passing cars, but they both agreed that it didn't seem to be from car lights or another reflection. Two other investigators were sitting up in the balcony and said they saw a shadow move across the bench on the other side of the room. They also thought they heard a sigh while sitting there, but they weren't positive and couldn't confirm what they heard. The next day, when they reviewed their audio, they heard the sigh right after they talked about seeing the shadow across the room. The EVP seemed to validate what they thought they had heard the night before.

Photo Evidence
from the Opera House

The Opera House is full of dust. Nobody will disagree with me about this statement. It is very old and very, very dusty, so taking pictures in the building can be quite a challenge. There have been many visitors over the years to the Opera House, and thousands of photos have been taken. People will take photos in the building and will send them to the L.A.C. staff, noting orbs in the photos or other anomalies. Mostly people see dust, but the photos do make compelling pictures sometimes.

As many times as we have been to the Opera House conducting investigations and other events, we have taken hundreds and hundreds of photos, if not thousands. Most of the photos that come into question when we review them have to be discounted because of the dust factor. The upstairs has been cleaned numerous times, and it seems almost impossible to get rid of the dust there, even though people have tried over and over again. My view on orbs is that they are fun to look at in photos, but I don't consider them to be evidence of a haunting or spirit activity. Some actual orbs might be a collection of energy, but there is no way to prove that beyond a shadow of doubt. So for now, I will stick to believing that they are mostly dust, moisture, lens reflection, or another camera-related objects. I must say, though, that even though I hold to this belief, I think that some orbs can in fact be more than dust balls. If they appear more solid in color and seem to be brighter than most dust orbs, it just might be an actual orb—something to consider and analyze.

Sandra, the team's lead investigator, and Bill, the team's technical specialist, like to take a lot of photos. While I am more interested in using my audio recorders and doing EVP research, they enjoy doing research when it comes to photographs. I must say it does work out well for the team as a whole.

There are a few orb photos that I want to share with you, as well as a couple of mist and shadow pictures that were taken at the Opera House.

What to Look for With Orb Photos

Orb photos can be tricky at times. Here are some tips for analyzing orbs in photos.

Look for solid orbs that are not transparent in nature.

Does the orb emit it's own light from within? If so, it's more likely to be an actual orb and not dust.

If there are numerous orbs in the photo-it's likely dust. Just one or two orbs and you are more likely to have the real thing.

Some Tips for Photographing Orbs

Take test shots so you know what dust looks like on your camera.

Do not photograph for orbs in the rain, while it's snowing, or in extremely dusty environments.

Do not photograph for orbs near a person who is smoking-this can lead to false-positives.

If you are in colder weather, hold your breath when taking the picture so as to not have a false-positive 'mist' photo as a result.

Pay attention to your surroundings and write down any shiny objects in the location. Sometimes a reflection can be deceiving.

I like to share our photos on the website for people to look at. We do not state that what we see in the photos is paranormal, because that is something that would be difficult to back up most of the time. We leave that up to the eye of the beholder, because everyone has their own beliefs about what they see. Here are few photos that have come from the Opera House, along with a short description of each photo.

RESEARCH

Because of the availability of the Opera House for continued investigation, we have been able to conduct research that is not usually possible for other locations. It's a wonderful place for research because the activity is mild and doesn't interfere with the daily activities and events that are held there. We don't have to worry that doing our research practices will produce negative effects, because we do respectful research, many times asking for the spirits there to give us a hand. I know that might sound very odd, but I have done it more than once, and I am not ashamed to admit it. I view the spirits in this building as my friends, and again, I know that the spirits there are friendly and enjoy having us around, and I feel very comfortable when I am there.

The acoustics in the building are just fantastic, which could be why our recordings from there are so amazing. Since there hasn't been anyone performing on the stage (no major performances, although a few people have done some minor performing) in roughly thirty years, we wanted to see what would happen if we got up on the stage and 'pretended' to perform.

We suspected nothing would come of it, and this was the case this time. But trying is a part of ghost hunting and our group always tries to leave no stone uncovered—especially since performing venues as a whole often have both audience and performer connections to the other side. Our theory was that if we did some performing on the stage, perhaps some of those from the other side would join in with us. On the other hand,

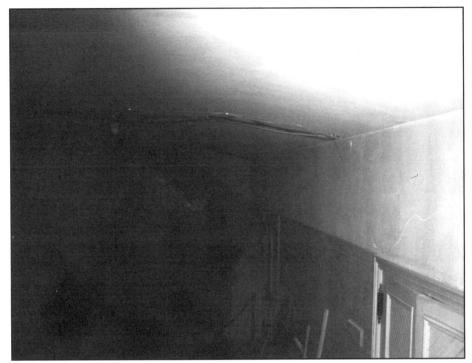

This photo was taken by Sandra in the same spot as the photo with the black mist shown on pages 140 and 141. As you can see, the photo is very dark on the left side compared to the right side. This was not her finger. If this were her finger, it wouldn't be black, and it wouldn't encompass such a large portion of the picture. The photos before and after this one showed no signs of a black shadow. The shadow in this picture was also taken on the same night as the black mist picture.
Courtesy of Sandra Kittle.

we weren't sure if they might become upset with us being on their stage. At any rate, another investigator and I got up on the stage one night and read a short play from a play book that I'd found at the local library. I must admit that I felt a bit silly doing this, but my curiosity was stronger than my feeling of silliness. For about ten to fifteen minutes, we stood on the stage reading from the book, while the other investigators watched and took pictures. Unfortunately, our experiment yielded no results. Since spirits usually know what we are thinking and doing, I am sure that they were 'on to us' and were probably laughing at our antics the whole time. But hey, it was worth a shot, right?

I have also done some experimentation with the K2 meter, which is basically an EMF reader that lights up when it picks up electromagnetic fields. The K2 meter has also been tested for use as a spirit communication device, by telling the spirits to flash the lights in a certain manner to answer questions (for example: flash once for *yes*, twice for *no*). And one of our investigators seemed to be getting some feedback from the spirits when she used the meter. On one episode of *"Ghost Hunters"* on the Sci-Fi channel, Chris Fleming, a well-known psychic medium and the person who seemed to make the K2 more public by using it at various investigations, asked questions to the spirits while a member from Ghost Hunters held the meter. It seemed to be answering as Chris asked the questions, lights flashing in the 'yes' and 'no' manner that he had set up. I have used the K2 meter on several occasions but I have not formed a solid opinion on it. The button on the meter has to be held down at all times, and this has led to discussions about how the user's hand movements could affect the results. I heard recently that the meter has been adapted and used with a switch that turns it on and off, so the investigator no longer has to hold it down while using it. This would take away the questions about interference from the investigator holding it during use.

Other research we conducted here involved some EVP research regarding how spirits like to communicate with us, and how they do it. Since we are there so often, I do believe that it makes a difference in the evidence that can be collected, and we are still studying various theories surrounding EVPs, photos, and videos as well. It is very nice to find a place where you can conduct research over a longer length of time, because most people know that spirits don't work on command and you never know what will happen during an investigation. Many times, nothing happens, and that is to be expected when heading into an investigation. Then there are those times when it seems that all hell might break loose and you will be caught right in the middle of it!

This photo was taken by Sandra during one of our investigations. She was either alone, or Bill was standing next to her. Everyone else on the team except for one person coming down the stage stairs was back near the ticket booth area, which is in the next room. As you can see, she aimed the camera directly towards the stage. This orb is very interesting because it is so bright and large in shape. You don't see many other orbs in the photo. In fact, there is only one smaller orb on the left-hand side, down towards the bottom of the picture. It is much more transparent than the large orb, and I would attribute this to dust floating around near the floor. The larger orb seems to have some dimension to it and as you can see it's much more solid than the smaller orb.
Courtesy of Sandra Kittle.

This photo was taken by Bill back behind the stage. On this night, the projector screen was pulled down and he had been sitting on the floor at the back of the stage doing some EVP work. The new psychic we were working with had actually channeled a woman before Bill went back here. He also captured an EVP during the time that he was sitting on the stage. This photo is interesting because of the number of orbs in the photo that seem to be lined up in a row. Along with the orbs you can see what looks like a beam of light where the orbs are. There weren't any flashlights shining at the stage when he took this picture, and subsequent photos didn't show any orbs. *Courtesy of Bill Kittle.*

This is a picture that was taken by Sandra back by the ticket booth. She was standing on one set of stairs when she took the photo, and she was aiming at the 'haunted staircase.' If you look on the left-hand side, you will see a darker area in the photograph which seems to be a black mist coming from the door of the ticket booth room and heading towards the stairs. The photo before and after this showed no signs of any black mist.
Courtesy of Sandra Kittle.

MORE RECENT ACTIVITY

Since I am a volunteer at the Opera House now and have become friends with some of the Board of Directors from the L.A.C. and other volunteers there, I hear about it when something odd has happened at there that cannot be explained. Since beginning this book, a few recent reports of strange things have been told to me by some of the Board Members. Lindsay Root told me that while filming an episode of Hub TV, a girl had an experience on the stage with her cello. She and her musical partner were on the stage warming up their instruments for the show. Later, while actually watching the episode of Hub TV, a local cable show about Howell and surrounding areas, I heard Brent Earl, the producer and host of the show, mention that a cello hadn't been played on the stage for over thirty years. It seems that when this girl began warming up her cello, the spirits weren't too thrilled with her playing it on the stage—either that, or they were trying to show off for the camera in the room at the time. The girl said that when she tried to warm up, something kept pushing the arm she used to hold her bow, like something was trying to knock it out of her hand. It seemed to be quite an experience for her, but she didn't give the impression of being too rattled by it either.

Another recent incident involved Sharon Fisher, Sales Manager for the Opera House. Sharon works long and hard hours renting out the first floor to people and sometimes is in the building alone. On one recent occasion when a wedding reception was taking place, the wedding party had taken photos upstairs on the stage and the projection screen had been unrolled. Later on that night, around 2 am, Sharon and another person rolled the screen back up to its normal position. She said that when she came back the next morning and went upstairs, the screen was unrolled.

When she told me about this, she said, "I asked around and nobody is claiming that they messed with the screen between the time I left and came back that morning." When I discussed what had happened with Lindsay Root, he said that the screen is pulled up and held in place by a rope that is wound around a rod on the stage. He said it was possible that perhaps a temperature change caused the rope to slip on the rod and that let the screen fall back down, but he said it wasn't probable because the screen is so heavy and its a chore to get it to move up and down.

I must admit that I found the recent activity odd because they normally don't experience these types of things in the building. One factor could be that there are more people in the building these days with the bottom floor being rented out and so much traffic in and out. Then I wondered if the ghosts were going to show off now, knowing I was writing a book and was going to include their story. If the latter is the reason, they got their wish! It's always validating when other people outside of our group experience things at the Opera House because it just lends a bit more mystery to the building and then we aren't the only ones talking about the spirits who reside in this wonderful place.

10

PARANORMAL TIPS

Throughout this book, I have gone over a few definitions and terms that relate to ghosts and ghost hunting, but I would also like to give you some other commonly-used definitions and tips that can point you in the right direction and give you some more helpful information when it comes to protocols and procedures used during paranormal investigations. Because we are dealing with the paranormal, some things cannot be proven and there may be differing opinions on what the definition of a ghost or spirit is, but I will use the most common terms in the glossary at the end of the book that are accepted my most investigators.

BEGINNERS GHOST HUNTING TIPS

Before you run out and try to be the best ghost hunter on the block, there are a few things that you need to be aware of and keep in mind. Ghost hunting isn't something that you should do for fun and kicks. I prefer to use the term paranormal investigator or paranormal researcher to define what I do. I will give you some tips on how to begin your journey into the world of paranormal research so that you can avoid some common errors when venturing out on your own.

RESEARCH, RESEARCH, RESEARCH

I cannot stress enough the importance of research that should be done when embarking out as a paranormal investigator, or even for a general enthusiast who is fascinated by ghosts and ghostly goings-on. When it comes to research about the paranormal, there is a wealth of information that can be found in books, on the Internet, and from other sources such as local groups in your area. Many of the groups hold special events where you can learn about the basics of ghost hunting, and some also offer more advanced lectures and feature speakers from the paranormal community who have been researching the paranormal for many years. Depending on what area you are most interested in (EVP work, parapsychology, etc.), you can narrow down your search and go from there.

A few authors that you might want to check out are Loyd Auerbach, Troy Taylor, and Jeff Belanger, who are all well-known and respected in this field. Troy Taylor has a book that is geared toward the ghost hunter called The Ghost Hunter's Guidebook—The Essential Guide to Investigating Ghosts & Hauntings. There are many fabulous books and articles that you can read to gain a better perspective on ghost hunting, running your own paranormal group, and a host of other paranormal topics.

After you have a bit of research under your belt, you can try to get your feet wet. Outdoor locations can be good, because you have more space to work with and more opportunity to try out your equipment. But there is one tip that I want to give about cemeteries before I go into more depth with the rest of my suggestions about ghost hunting. You should always get permission before going to any cemetery after dark. Most of the cemeteries close at dusk and with the rise of vandalism these days, you need to protect yourself and make sure that the local authorities know you will be there and have given you permission beforehand. Research the township, town, or city where the cemetery is located to find the right contact for gaining permission. Most times, this can be done on the Internet. If you don't have any luck searching that way, you can call the local police office for the area and sometimes that is the only call that is necessary. If not, they can point you in the right direction.

Don't Jump Ahead

If you are trying to start your own paranormal group, don't jump ahead of things and try to investigate a home or business right from the get-go. This is one time when I do recommend starting off in cemeteries or other outside locations so that you and any potential members of your group can become familiar with equipment and procedures that are used when conducting investigations. Being at an outside location gives you the freedom to walk around freely and talk to the other people with you about how you should set-up equipment, doing test runs, etc. It is a good idea to become familiar with all of your equipment so that you know what each piece is used for and how it works. This saves time and frustration in the long run.

Equipment Basics

You don't need a thermal imaging camera or other fancy equipment to perform investigations. For starters, a basic camera and audio recorder is all that you need, along with common sense and your own intuition. These are basic tools for ghost hunting that can go a long way for quite some time. Thermal imaging cameras, fancy video cameras, and other equipment that you see on television are very expensive and aren't necessary when you are starting out. They can be helpful, but certainly aren't the only way to capture evidence.

You can use a **35mm camera with film or a digital camera**. Both work and some investigators use both because they like to have the negatives that come with 35mm pictures once developed. Any kind of anomaly would then show up on the negative, leaving less room for debate on what was captured. This is a good thing, but developing film each time can be costly since you need to take a lot of pictures at each investigation. It is also good to take two subsequent pictures in a row so you have something to use as a comparison, should you pick something up in one of them.

Audio recorders are an invaluable tool for research and are by far my favorite piece of equipment. You can use an analog recorder which uses cassette tapes, either regular or micro-cassettes, or one of the newer digital recorders that are on the market. I personally use both, and tend to favor the cassette recorder for it's simplicity, but it is a matter of personal choice as to which one you use. Sometimes, I think I get more EVPs with the cassette recorder, and it's a common theory that perhaps the magnetic tape in the recorder can pick up spirit voices easier than the digital because the digital does not use a tape at all. Again, it's all a matter of preference and what you feel most comfortable using.

Video cameras are another common piece of technological equipment that we use. You can use them while walking through a location, or use a tripod to set them up in one room while you investigate other areas of the building. We like to use them in areas where activity is reported, say in a bedroom of a home. We will put the video camera in the bedroom and then shut the door. This way we know that anything we might capture on the video wouldn't be caused by one of our investigators since the room was closed off.

Video cameras come in many models with different functions. The most helpful function as an investigator is night vision, which gives the camera the capability of filming in the dark. If your video camera does not have night vision, you can take a small flashlight and secure it on the top of the camera to give some light in the room without it being overwhelming. This works for smaller spaces, but does not work as well in larger areas because the flashlight beam will only travel so far out in front of it. You can also purchase the cylinder security types of cameras and hook them to laptops, as seen on many paranormal shows on television. You can usually hook up four cameras or more at once if you have the right equipment for doing that. This would be the easiest method so that you can have one person watching the activity on the cameras at the same time while sitting at the laptop or monitor.

EMF detectors are used by many paranormal groups to pick up on electromagnetic fields. Sometimes high electromagnetic fields can cause paranoia and other emotions which can be mistaken for spirit activity, therefore, they are good to have in homes so this can be tested or ruled out. A common theory is that spirits use energy to manifest, so a high EMF reading along with a personal experience by an investigator or something on audio or film could signify that a spirit is present. I don't recommend that you deem a place haunted because it has high EMF readings. Most electrical equipment gives off high readings, so you need to do base readings at the location before you begin your investigation so you will know what the normal reading number would be and have something to compare later readings to, should you get a high spike on the meter.

Another theory about spirits is that because they need to 'take' energy in order to manifest in any way, the temperature in the room will drop when they are present because they are using up the energy and heat. Temperature readings can be taken with equipment like laser **thermometers and other basic temperature readers**. Again, use discretion when using this tool and keep in mind what I said above about EMF detectors.

Other things that you need for an investigation include **paper and pen** for writing down any personal experiences. You can find small pads of paper in any general store and they are easy to carry with you and don't take up much space. If you are doing a home investigation, you will also want **permission forms** for the homeowners to sign allowing you or your group to investigate, any **interview questionnaires** to help you interview them and any other papers that pertain to the investigation.

Extra batteries are also a must-have in case your batteries go dead in your equipment. Batteries can also be drained by spirits who are trying to gather up energy to manifest. I like to use rechargeable batteries because they seem to last longer than regular batteries. Some equipment with rechargeable batteries might not work properly, if, for example, it is an older recorder or camera, so check before you leave the house so you know what you will need for each piece of equipment.

First-aid kits are something you should take along if you are going to be outside in the dark or in an older building such as an old prison, hospital, etc. Many times, these locations can pose hazards such as sharp objects, rocks or bricks that can scrape your skin, fall on you, or something else that can hurt you. It is a wise idea to carry Band-Aids and antiseptic in case you need them.

Another must would be **flashlights** for all investigators because many investigations are done in the dark—even though you don't have to conduct them in the dark for them to be effective.

Protocols and Rules

If you are starting a paranormal group, you will want to have some basic protocols and rules for the group as a whole. From the very beginning, decide what kind of group you want to have, and what your goal and focus as a group will be. It can be hard in the beginning to find others who you get along with and who you think will fit into your group. Having a group means you are a team and that you will work together to get things done. (Some people are not made for teamwork and just like to do things on their own, and that is fine also.) It can take some time to find the right people for your group, but you will find them in time. When you do, you will want to set up some protocols on how you want to run your investigations.

When it comes to my group, we are more laid back in how we do our investigations. I have never been one for mapping things out and going too overboard with paperwork and such. I am not saying that we don't document things, because we do, but I give my investigators more freedom then some other groups do. I do have some basic protocols and basic rules such as:

> No drinking before or during investigation,
> No disrespect to anyone in the group or any clients, and
> Projecting a professional manner when on any investigation.

I think most things are common sense, so I don't get too bogged down with telling people in your new organization what to do. For my group, members will ask me where to set up cameras and other equipment, and I will tell them where I think we should put them, and then ask their opinions as to what they think. I want everyone in the group to be involved in what we are doing, and enjoy themselves at the same time. Laying down too many rules or trying to dictate all the time does not always work out for the best.

Some people like a more structured group and some people like a group, like mine, which is more laid back. If you are totally lost on what type of protocols you should have, you can ask other groups what they have in place and then incorporate your own ideas into them. The reason my group likes to be more relaxed is because it allows the opportunity for everyone to participate in some research that might not have otherwise happened if things were more strict. If they want to try out an experiment, they are free to do so as long as it is within normal boundaries and won't hurt anyone at the location. Brainstorming beforehand can be a good thing also, so that when you get ready to investigate, you won't waste time and can get right to setting up your equipment so you can get started.

Dealing With Clients

Once you have some experience under your belt and you are ready to do home investigations, you have to understand how to deal with the clients in the home. First contact with them can be a phone call or an email asking you for help, whether they just have questions they want to ask or they want you to come to conduct an investigation at their home. When you talk to them, the most important thing to remember is that you must listen, and to try to be objective about what they are telling you. Many times, they will have stories that might seem to be way *out there*, or irrational. Sometimes, for the minor things, you can suggest explanations as to what you think might be happening, such as high electromagnetic fields within the home.

High electromagnetic fields in the home can cause symptoms such as paranoia, where one might feel that someone (or a ghost) is watching your every move, nausea, headaches, fatigue, and a rash of other physical ailments, some of which can be pretty severe.

You'll want to have a paper and pen nearby while you are speaking to them on the phone so that you can document what they are telling you about their experiences. Some groups make a special appointment to go and conduct an in-home interview separately, before the initial investigation, but I don't always work in this manner. If the home is a longer distance from where I am, I will ask them many of the interview questions over the phone to provide a head start. I also find that by doing it this way, they become more comfortable with you right from the beginning. Often times I talk to them more than once, before we even step foot in the house. They usually have many questions they want answered, and just feel relieved to be able to talk to someone who doesn't think they are crazy when they tell them their experiences.

There is quite a bit of psychology that can come into play when you are dealing with clients and paranormal investigations. You'll need to try to get a feel for what type of person your client is, while at the same time not being judgmental about them. Do they seem to be of stable mental health? Do they have stories of previously living in haunted homes? Do you think they have looked for logical reasons as to what might be causing the phenomena they are experiencing? All of these questions and more can pop up when you are speaking to clients about the activities they are recounting to you.

You have to be able to talk to them compassionately and sincerely. This makes it easier on them and by gaining their trust you will receive even more information that will be a big help to both you and them at the same time.

Make sure that between your quest for scientific proof and your protocols, the homeowners and clients don't get lost in the mix. I hear that some groups ask the homeowners to leave their own homes while they are conducting an investigation. I can understand requiring this if activity seems to be negative in nature, but with most investigations, this is not necessary. Many times spirits can also be attached to one person in the household. If that person is not present during the investigation, will the spirit be present? This is something to think about as you plan your investigation.

Since I am not into proving paranormal activity, our interactions are more in-tuned with our clients' needs, and our investigations reflect that because we usually have the homeowners present when we are there. I know that if I had five or more people coming into my home—who I don't know—I would be very uncomfortable leaving them there at night while I wasn't there. I would not agree to this and I don't think anyone should have to make this decision. I find it beneficial to have them in the home. They are the people who live there, and they are the ones experiencing the activity, so they need to be there when we are. I usually do recommend that the children leave the house because we never know what will happen during an investigation and I would not want to scare any child any more than they might already be. The parents usually agree to this wholeheartedly so children are typically taken somewhere else for the night.

If the homeowners don't want to be in the house while we investigate because they are too frightened that our being there could stir things up, then by all means, they can leave the house. I base each investigation according to what my conversations with the clients have shown, and go from there. Do what you feel is best for them at all times.

You might be asking yourself, "Well if my clients are there, won't that taint my evidence?" No, not really. I ask them if they would like to stay in one room while we investigate, or stay with us as we investigate. Many of our clients are also interested in the paranormal and they are fascinated with the whole concept of investigations, so they want to stay with us and investigate also. This is fine with me and we have worked with clients this way many times. I usually ask them to please not whisper, so we don't end up thinking that we have captured a spirit whispering when it was one of them instead. We are not familiar enough with the sounds of their voices to distinguish their whispers on audio. I tell them that if they are going to speak, to do so in their regular speaking voices. I also let them ask their own questions during EVP work if they want to. I do ask that they not talk excessively, as this *can* taint the audio, but I do allow them to talk during recording because we feel this can actually help us out when trying to lure the spirits to communicate.

THINK OUTSIDE THE BOX

Always remember to think outside the box when you are involved with paranormal investigations. Don't try to do things just because other groups are doing them and you think their way is the only way. Don't throw away spiritual aspects of investigating because you are all about science, and vice versa. As I have said before, the paranormal is not a proven field and there are many theories and ways to do things. There aren't any experts in this field, so don't get too wrapped up in if you are right or wrong, because there *is* no right or wrong, only different matters of opinion and different ways of running investigations. Remember who you are as an individual and why you began your paranormal quest to begin with. Don't forget who you are or ever sacrifice that to gain something you might not even want in the long run.

If there are theories you want to test, then do it. You never know what will happen when you think outside the box and test things out. If you are interested in making new gadgets for investigations and have the know-how, then go ahead and do it. You don't have anything to lose other than some patience once and a while. If you are more interested in the spiritual aspect and how spirits relate and communicate with us, then work from that end of the field. You will discover what you and your group can offer to people when it comes to paranormal research, and you will find that as time goes on, your interests might change from one thing to another. Perhaps you will become more involved with EVP research than you were before, or you will change and want to study electromagnetic fields, moon cycles and phases, or how weather might play a factor in spirit activity. Just remember to ask yourself a few questions as you begin and as you continue to grow in the field.

Why are you really doing this? Is it for your own interest? Is it to try to prove to other people that the paranormal exists? Is it to help out clients and educate the public? Or is it all of the above. If you know why you are doing investigations and know what your beliefs are and where you stand, then the rest of it will fall into place as you go along. Don't become worried about your group logo, your group name, your website, and other minor details in the beginning, just go out and *learn as much as you can.* The more you know, the better prepared you are, whether it comes to equipment, gaining permissions to do investigations, or dealing with clients. Respect is a big thing to me and I use respect for both the clients, people in my group, and the spirits that we are trying to gain some insight from. I am sure that there are many times when the spirits are wondering why we are trying so hard to find out more about the other side, and other times when they are simply just laughing at us. But I also know that they are there to help us understand, and if we all work together with each other and with the spirits, we will continue to evolve in the paranormal field and we will continue to learn more each day about the answers we are searching for.

GLOSSARY

Angels
Spiritual beings who have never lived an earthly life. They assist in both the spiritual and physical earth world.

Apparition
A spirit/ghost that manifests enough energy to appear in what seems to be a human form with a body or shape to it.

Apport
An object that seems to appear out of nowhere with no reasonable explanation as to where it came from.

Automatic Writing
The ability to write messages or text without consciously being aware of what is being written. Often times automatic writing is done with assistance from spirits, spirit guides, Angels, and other spirit beings.

Channeling
Receiving messages from spirit beings on the other side. Channeling can also involve going into a trance state where the spirit can use the channeler's body, voice, etc. There are semi and full trance states.

Clairaudience
Receiving both spirit and non-spirit related messages through hearing sounds and/or voices.

Clairvoyance
Receiving messages through visions and images. Some people also receive messages while holding objects or touching them with their hands—also known as psychometry.

Clairsentience
The term used for receiving general and or spirit messages through feeling or clear thought/knowing.

Crisis Apparition

When a person is seen in apparition form either before, during, or after an event such as an illness, tragic event, or death.

DejaVu

When someone feels that current events taking place with them or around them have previously happened before.

Demonic Possession

When an evil spirit takes over a person. Demonic possessions can also come in the form of demonic hauntings, where the evil spirit might haunt or take over a house or building.

Ectoplasm

Appearing at times to look like mist or smoke, ectoplasm can be seen coming from people who channel spirits and it also appears often in pictures. Ectoplasm can form shapes as well.

EMF Detector (Electromagnetic Field)

Used by paranormal investigators to pick up on electromagnet fields. Ghosts are believed to use electromagnetic energy to make sounds, move objects, or appear in apparition form.

EVP (Electromagnetic Voice Phenomena)

The ability to pick up spirit voices on electrical devices such as tape recorders, answering machines, televisions, and other electrical devices.

Empathy

The ability to feel another persons emotions such as happiness, pain, illness, etc.

Exorcism

A religious ceremony or ritual that is used to drive out evil spirits that are possessing someone.

ESP (Extra Sensory Perception)

The ability to use one's "sixth sense" to pick up on information about people or events.

Ghost
Term used most often to describe the appearance/presence of a disembodied person who is no longer living.

Guide
Also known as spirit guide or spiritual guide. Spirit guides assist people on their spiritual journeys and on a daily basis as well.

Haunted/Haunting
This is a term used to describe spirit/ghost activity at a location such as moving objects, unexplained sounds, apparitions, and other paranormal events that take place at a particular location for extended periods of time.

Medium (Spirit Communicator)
Someone who can communicate with spirits and receive/pass on messages from spirits to those who are still alive.

Orb
Often seen on pictures or video, orbs are believed by some to be energy and by others to be spirit beings who have manifested in orb form. Orbs are typically round when seen on video or film.

Paranormal
Used to describe things that do not appear to have 'normal' explanations or scientific proof.

Thermal Camera
A camera that shows cold/hot spots coming off people or objects.

BIBLIOGRAPHY

Arnt, Les E. *The Bay County Story—From Footpaths to Freeways.* Bay City, Michigan :Les E. Arndt, 1982.

Butterfield, George Ernest. *Bay County Past and Present.* Bay County, Michigan: C & J Gregory, 1918.

Crittenden, A. Riley. *A History of the Village and Township of Howell, Michigan.* Howell, Michigan: Livingston Tidings Print, 1911

Danelek, J. Allan. *The Case For Ghosts: An Objective Look at the Paranormal.* Woodbury, Minnesota: Llewellyn Publications, 2006.

Godfrey, Linda S.,Moran, Mark, Sceurman, Mark. *Weird Michigan: Your Travel Guide to Michigan's Local Legends and Best Kept Secrets.* New York, New York: Sterling Publishing Co., Inc, 2006.

Rogers, D. Laurence. *Paul Bunyan: How a Terrible Timber Fella Became a Legend.* Bay City, Michigan: Historical Press, Inc., 1993.

Other Resources

Ancestry Magazine, The Truth About Folk Heroes, Vol. 21, No.2, March 1, 2003: www.ancestry.com

Bay City Convention and Visitors Bureau. www.tourbaycitymi. org

Bay-Journal www.bay-journal.com

Ghosts of the Prairie. www.prairieghosts.com

National Register of Historic Places. Site No. 71001018, 1971, Fletcher Site, www.nps.gov/history/nr

Paranormal Researchers in Southeastern Michigan. www. ghostprism.com

State Theatre. www.statetheatrebaycity.com

Taylor, Troy. Haunted Michigan, Haunted Light Houses, 1998: www.prairieghosts.com.

The Opera House, Home of the Livingston Arts Council. www. theoperahouse.us

INDEX